NEO-
FUNDAMENTALISM

NEO-

FUNDAMENTALISM

The Humanist Response

PRESENTED BY

The Academy of Humanism

PROMETHEUS BOOKS
Buffalo, New York

Contents

The Growth of
Fundamentalism Worldwide

Paul Kurtz

I

In the late nineteenth century, it was widely believed by the leading intellectuals that superstitious religions would decline and that, with increased education, improved standards of health, and economic well-being, the classical religious orthodoxies would be replaced by a humanist civilization based upon reason and science. But, although the technological revolution has made great progress, shrinking the globe, facilitating travel and communication between peoples, and raising the standards of living and education worldwide, tribal and religious loyalties have persisted. Although some denominations, influenced no doubt by humanism, have been liberalized, have attempted to accommodate themselves to modern science and democracy, and have even promoted the expansion of the frontiers of freedom and progress, others have doggedly resisted the humanist agenda. In particular, there has been a growth of neo-fundamentalism worldwide.

The emergence of neo-fundamentalism in America is a puzzling phenomenon. From 30 to 40 percent of Americans consider themselves to be born-again Christians, and if one adds the adherents of traditional Roman Catholicism and Con-

7

servative and Orthodox Jews, this coalition begins to comprise a majority of citizens.

Moreover, as neo-fundamentalism makes steady inroads in American life, there is a massive missionary effort under way worldwide, much of it financed by ultraconservative American religions and televangelists. The humanist movement has concentrated on developing its own rather fragile national humanist organizations, largely, although not exclusively, in the Western world. Critical of colonialism, humanists have not made any concerted effort to export their philosophy to the third world and have paid little attention to the extensive evangelizing efforts of fundamentalist Christian churches now going on in the developing countries.

In a recent article in *Christianity Today*, Patrick J. Johnstone, international research secretary of the Worldwide Evangelization Crusade, claims that "the last ten years have been the most dramatic harvest the world has ever seen" and that, although the membership of all churches is growing, the evangelical, fundamentalist, and pentecostal churches have made the widest gains especially outside of Western Europe and North America.[1] This rapid growth is due to two factors: (1) the increase in population, and (2) the intensive evangelical efforts at conversion. Unfortunately, many countries do not have a scientific, philosophical, skeptical, or free thought tradition and are easy prey for dogmatic religious systems.

According to C. Peter Wagner, professor at the Fuller Theological Seminary School of World Missions in Pasadena, California, "the most massive church growth is in China."[2] This is surprising to many Western observers. Although it is difficult to estimate the number of new Christian converts in China, claims range anywhere from 5 million to 100 million. Christian Communities, Ltd., of Hong Kong, maintains that from 35 to 50 million is a "credible" estimate. If this is the case, it would be remarkable, given the previous hostility of the Chinese Marxist regime to religion.

In other parts of Asia, the growth of Christianity has been especially rapid. In South Korea, 24 percent of the population is now Christian. In the Philippines, at one time largely Roman Catholic, the Protestant churches have been growing by 10 percent a year since 1975, and church leaders have announced that they plan to build 46,000 new churches by the year 2000. Great efforts have been made for over a century, to Christianize Japan, with little effect, though some missionaries now claim that progress is now being made. The number of Christian writers in Japan is proportionately very large compared with the small church attendance, and this has had an acknowledged impact on ethics and values. Christians today hold leading positions in many Japanese academic institutions, including the presidency of a respected Tokyo University. Many Japanese, imitative of the West, now even celebrate Christmas.

In Africa, south of the Sahara, there has been a rapid growth of Christianity in recent years. I visited West Africa in 1984. Although the president of the former French colony had recently converted to Islam, television and newspaper reports often told of Christian missionary efforts, and evangelical supporters were welcomed to the presidential palace with considerable fanfare. Donald McGavran, founder of the Fuller School of World Missions, maintains that sub-Saharan Africa is becoming a "Christian land mass, just as Europe did between the years of 200 and 1000."[3,4]

In South America, the Protestant churches have also been attracting millions of converts from Christo-pagan religions and Roman Catholicism. In Brazil, the Protestant population has grown from 6 percent twenty-five years ago to nearly 20 percent today. Similarly, the Mormon Church, Jehovah Witnesses, and other sects have made great inroads in South America, especially in Brazil. Some 80 percent of Brazilians are nominal Catholics and heavily influenced by spiritism. Whereas forty years ago only 8 percent of the Brazilians were practicing primitive spiritism, today it is estimated that 60 percent do. When I was interviewed on a leading television program in Brazil, the producer, who was something of a skeptic, told me he was trying in some modest way to counteract the tremendous growth of belief in spiritism and the paranormal.

In Argentina, the Protestant churches have grown by nearly 7 percent a year since 1980. One might argue that it is well and good that such Roman Catholic bastions are having competition, that perhaps this is the beginning of a new Protestant reformation. Unfortunately, the evangelicals who are gaining ground are not necessarily liberalizing forces; more often they are reactionary movements, ever more literalist and fundamentalist in their interpretations of the Bible and morality. As Jorge J. E. Gracia pointed out in the summer issue of *Free Inquiry* magazine, Latin America has had no substantial tradition of religious skepticism, and whatever there was is now in eclipse.

Interestingly, John Paul II has taken the church backward in doctrinal dogma. In Israel, Orthodox Jews rail against secularists and protest the secular aspects of modern Israeli life. We have seen a similarly unsettling revival of Muslim fundamentalism and a counterrevolution against modernist tendencies in Iran, Pakistan, Lebanon, Egypt, and elsewhere, and Islam has been winning large numbers of converts in Asia and Africa. Moreover, there has been a growth in bizarre new cults and a surprising recrudescence—in this scientific age—of paranormal belief systems, including belief in psychic phenomena and astrology.

II

What does the term *fundamentalism* mean? As I use it, it refers to any movement or attitude that stresses strict and literal adherence to a set of fundamental principles or values. A fundamentalist is one who Eric Hoffer has called "a true believer," i.e., one who professes belief in a creed, doctrine, dogma, code, or ideology that he accepts unreservedly and without question. His commitment is firm, inflexible, and unwavering. These principles are taken as absolute, unchanging, eternal. The system of fundamentalist belief, at least in theory if not in practice, is used as a guide for all aspects of life and encourages the development of a pathological authoritarian personality.

Fundamentalists often seek to use the power of the state to compel conformity in belief and to suppress dissent. They are sometimes willing to use any methods at their disposal to achieve their aims, even violence or terror—all justifiable in the name of God. There is a battle, they believe, between the children of light (their side) and the forces of darkness (the enemy). A kind of self-righteous moral fanaticism can result; for, since the true believer is doing God's work, he believes that he is justified in opposing his enemies in any way he can.

The contrary, humanistic attitude repels fundamentalists. If humanists stress free inquiry and the need for an open mind, fundamentalists feel it should be kept shut. For humanists, knowledge is tentative, fallible, hypothetical; for fundamentalists, infallible and certain. Humanists are self-critical and skeptical, even about their own premises. Fundamentalist never waver in their firm conviction that Righteousness and Truth are on their side. For humanists, tolerance is essential; fundamentalists are intolerant of any criticism of the Sacred Faith. Humanists can live with ambiguity and uncertainty; fundamentalists cannot. Humanists respect individual liberty, uniqueness, freedom, diversity; fundamentalists cannot tolerate other people doing what they consider to be sinful or wicked and they have no use for differences, particularly in the area of moral belief and conduct. Humanists welcome change and find novelty interesting; they are willing to experiment and are open to new departures in thought and action. Fundamentalists are horrified by change and adamantly cling to old verities. Humanists want their children to develop on their own terms into complete persons and provide them with enriched education; fundamentalists insist that their children be molded to fit their own preconceived ideas and values, and any weakening of the faith in their children is viewed with fear. Humanists view truth (with a small *t*) as a product of an ongoing inquiry, tested by evidence and judged in the light of reason and experience. For fundamentalists, Truth is Absolute. Once pronounced, it is beyond revision. For humanists, morality is relative to human institutions and needs. They are willing to test moral principles and values by their observed consequences. Humanists believe in moral decency and moral virtues, but they judge ethical principles by how well they work in practice and by their contributions to human well-being. Fundamentalists derive their moral principles from revealed truth, as handed down in ancient times, and they are inflexible in their insistence that they are God's absolute commandments.

I have perhaps exaggerated the contrast between these two polarities; no doubt there are gradations within each of them. It should also be pointed out that it is possible for secularists to express narrow fundamentalist attitudes about their own cherished ideological principles. This is particularly true in the case of those who in the name of building a utopia are willing to suppress dissent. In any case, the persistence of fundamentalism is sufficiently prevelent in the world today that it threatens the further progress of humanism and the development of democracy, freedom, science, and reason.

III

Why do fundamentalist forces persist and indeed continue to gain ground, given the enormous technological and social changes going on? This is a broad question that I cannot hope to do full justice to here. I will mention only three possible explanations, although there are no doubt others.

The first is *sociological.* It maintains that religious institutions reflect underlying political, economic, cultural, social, and ethnic influences. The major religions that have survived are among the most venerable and surely the oldest institutions of human civilization: Judaism, Christianity, Islam, Buddhism, Hinduism, and Confucianism go back thousands of years and permeate the entire fabric of the demographic areas in which they are dominant. These religions play a stabilizing role because of ethnic inbreeding. They define the linguistic and cultural heritage of a group of people living and working together. There have been unsettling periods of conversion and change, however, as when Christianity swept through the pagan Roman Empire of the fourth century and overturned the competing Mithraic religion and when Islam conquered vast territories, displacing ancient Christian, Jewish, Berber, and other communities. Missionary efforts are ongoing, especially in pluralistic societies. Diverse sects and cults constantly seek to gain adherents at the fringes of the great religious institutions. At certain pivotal points in history, there are paradigmatic religious shifts of massive proportions, but these have been relatively infrequent, and the staying power of the classical religions is surprising, in spite of wars, revolutions, and even in the face of radical social change.

How could the incredible mythological tale about a dead and risen son of God, as outlined in the New Testament, have been accepted in the simple nomadic and agricultural culture of the Middle East of the first centuries C.E., the highly

sophisticated Hellenized Roman culture, feudal Europe, indus-
trialized capitalist societies, post-industrial technological
societies, and the diverse Asian and African cultures of today?
Similarly, why have so many Jews, the members of a be-
leaguered and persecuted minority, clung to their tribal Judaic
traditions, outlined in the Old Testament and the Torah, for
more than three thousand years, adapting themselves to widely
differing social contexts? And why did the Koran have an
unparalleled impact in the centuries following the death of
Muhammad, inundating lands from Western Africa on the
Atlantic, all the way to the Indus River and Indonesia in
the east? Why does it persist today in societies that are under-
going rapid transformations? Whenever atheists, skeptics, or
humanists have confidently proclaimed the death of God in
one generation it surprisingly reappears in the next, spurred
on by new waves of revivalist fervor.

There are no doubt sociological explanations that can
be given for this phenomenon. In times of uncertainty and
stress people seem to turn to God. The sudden upsurge of
religious hegemony can also be given a politico-military
explanation. The word of God becomes entrenched when it
is reinforced by the sword. When religious theocracies have
seized control of state power, have dictated the educational
system and legislated and enforced economic, legal, and moral
doctrine. Simplified political explanations by themselves do
not seem to suffice, however, for the classical religious institutions have survived wars and revolutions and have persisted
under widely different political conditions: oligarchical, mon-
archical, dictatorial, and democratic.

Is there an economic determinant that can explain the
growth and persistence of religious institutions? Christianity and
Judaism have prevailed in radically differing economic systems:
nomadic, agricultural, imperial, feudal, capitalist, and socialist.
The Dutch settlers of South Africa, the Australian outbackers,

and the cowboys of the American West left their established societies to create new ones, yet they brought with them their traditional religious belief-systems, adapted no doubt to frontier conditions. Was Marx then correct in his sociological interpretation of history, that religious institutions are a reflection of the underlying forces and relationships of production? An empirical study of what is happening in Eastern Europe, the Soviet Union, China, and other Marxist countries is of vital significance to this question: Has orthodox religiosity survived in socialist economies, or will it in time disappear? Marxism no doubt has had a powerful liberating role in its critique of corrupt economic and religious systems, which were often allied to maintain the status quo. Paradoxically, however, many theologians and priests today are in the forefront of national liberation movements in the third world. Moreover, some Marxist countries have replaced the *ancien régimes* with new forms of a nontheistic fundamentalist faith, especially when the dialectic laws of history are interpreted as a kind of Absolute Truth, and when a state apparatus is developed that seeks to suppress dissent or attempts to define ideological purity.

There is thus a second possible explanation for the persistence of religiosity, and that is the hypothesis that the roots of religion are *sociobiological.* E. O. Wilson of Harvard University, a member of the Academy of Humanism, argues that there are deep biological and genetic factors that contribute to social behavior, and that these function in similar ways in other species, which seem to display a kind of instinctive moral-altruistic behavior that enables them to live and function together.[5] If this is so, then, systems of religion, however false their beliefs may be, may have some survival value in the evolutionary process, for they would enable an inbreeding social group to cope with adversity; they offer solace and a way to overcome existential dispair and the tragic character of human existence. These religious systems thus have both psychological and sociological functions. Group survival depends upon the development of moral rules and regulations governing behavior; religions provide the transcendental support in terms of sanctions and rewards for morality. Religions also celebrate the rites of passage that are common to all human cultures: birth, puberty, marriage, death. They provide a basis for stability and continuity of the social group. The hypothesis is that those individuals who conform to the religious structures of the group and receive its balm are better able to survive and transmit this genetic disposition to their offspring.

Can human beings be described as *Homo religious?* Is there a "transcendental gene"? The pervasive character of religious institutions would seem for some to point in this direction. Nevertheless, I have some reservations about this explanation for the following reasons: Transcendental and theistic belief-systems are *absent* in significant portions of humankind. This does not deny that an ethical imperative built into the human species *may* be biogenetic, but I doubt that there is also a built-in transcendental imperative. First, not all cultures have displayed it in the same context as it appears in monotheistic religions. Second, if religion has a genetic source, then how do we explain the existence of anomic unbelievers? If belief in the transcendental were a universal constant in human nature, why are there dissident minorities in many societies who reject the appeal to the transcendental? Is this not evidence *against* there being a fixed genetic determinant?

Now I must say that my rejection of the genetic explanation has been chastened somewhat by my involvement in researching the paranormal during the past decade. As chairman of the Committee for the Scientific Investigation of Claims of the Paranormal, an international group of scientists and skeptics, I have been dismayed at the widespread prevalence of belief in the paranormal—that which allegedly cannot be explained scientifically by reference to normal or natural causes—for example, psychic phenomena, UFOlogy, and astrology. It is also a source of astonishment to discover that, when many people abandon the faith of their fathers, they or their children may flock to newer cults of mystery and transcendence. Moreover, belief in the paranormal, (so popular in today's media and science fiction fantasies) bears striking analogies to similar psychological and social processes discovered in the formation of the ancient religions. Moses, Jesus, Muhammad, Joseph Smith, and other prophets were not unlike paranormal conjurers and magicians like Eusapia Palladino and Uri Geller. Thus we may wonder whether the same transcendent fixation is simply reappearing in a new paranormal guise, and whether the fact that fraud and deception work is due to a naive gullibility rooted in a genetic tendency in the species.

Not necessarily, for in working closely with college students and adults in courses I have taught on the paranormal and parapsychology, I have found that extensive and in-depth examination of the evidence or lack of it can lead people to abandon their former beliefs in the paranormal and develop a skeptical attitude. The same thing is true of people who by critical examination are able to reject their former, deeply rooted religious beliefs; some even become atheists, agnostics, skeptics, or humanists. The process of deconversion, however, is often extremely torturous and difficult to achieve. For if there is not a genetic cause, there is at least a deep-seated tendency in the human breast for magical, occult, or supernatural thinking.

Thus I offer as a third explanation what I call the "transcendental temptation," that is, a tendency to believe in an unseen, hidden, supernormal world, that transcends the natural world of science and controls our destinies.[6] The transcendental temptation is both biological and social in origin and function. The transcendental temptation cannot be easily identified with determinate genetic structures, even though there are strong biopsychological and sociocultural urges present that tend to push human beings in the direction of acceptance of an occult or unseen universe and lead them to supplicate and worship dieties in the hope of achieving deliverance and salvation. The transcendental temptation is the source of the true believer's exclamation: "Only God can save us."

The best therapy for affliction by the transcendental temptation is scientific investigation and critical skeptical rationality. Since it is possible to overcome it, I do not think it is deterministically genetic. For human beings are able to transform mystery into understanding by discovering the natural causes at work. There has been a long and arduous struggle in human civilization to discover naturalistic, causal explanations for human suffering and tragedy—death, earthquakes, volcanoes, and plagues—that were otherwise inexplicable disasters historically attributed to occult causes.

Modern science is a relatively new phenomenon in human culture—only four centuries have passed since it began to develop. Yet even primitive man had to use cognitive thought to some extent. Critical intelligence or common sense is a prerequisite for coping with problems encountered in the environment, but learning to use it has been a slow process. The point is that scientific knowledge has expanded enormously our ability to understand and control nature and our concomitant sense of power. Thus, in spite of any biogenetic instinctive endowment, the gullibility to which we are prone, and the tendency to allow our passions and wishes to dictate our belief, we are still capable as a species of cognitive behavior. Critical intelligence can therefore have a profound and liberating effect. It can free us from blind ignorance or vain illusions about reality, and it can disabuse us of any lingering hankerings that we may have for simplified anthropocentric and anthropomorphic explanations of the universe.

The transcendental temptation has its source in still another dimension of human nature, our capacity for *creative imagination*. In a sense, human civilization is extra-natural; it is a product of *art, techné,* and *praxis*. It did not exist before men and women came onto the scene. Human culture is a product of our creative imagination spilling out into the world and changing the course of history. Civilization is the sum total of the visions and dreams bequeathed to us from earlier generations who overcame barriers, forged frontiers, made new discoveries, built roadways into the interiors, and erected palaces and cathedrals. Much of human society and culture no doubt develops unconsciously, but the civilizations that remain are the result of the plans and projects of human beings. We envision new worlds, which we discover or invent, and which we long to bring about. Religious institutions are also the result of the creative process. Overladen with mythology and fantasy, they are nonetheless products of the passionate yearnings and aspirations of human beings, the anticipations of what life could be like in an ideal world in which our fondest desires come true, a world in which those we loved in life will live again and be with us throughout eternity. This dream appeals to the imagination of every age: A transcendental universe is far more attractive and comforting than an impersonal or purposeless one. It is thus the union of the transcendental temptation with the creative imagination that produces religious poetry.

IV

It is time that I bring together the strands of my arguments and deal with the question, What is to be done? I would like to suggest some recommendations for the humanist movement by way of conclusion.

As a starting point, I believe that it is important that we embark on a major educational outreach worldwide, but especially in the third world—Latin America, Africa, and Asia. We cannot remain content to espouse our principles politely in the quiet cloisters of our own societies, but must meet head on the massive challenges in the developing countries of the world.

In one sense the historic expansion of Western countries—in its exploratory, imperialist, military, economic, and political phases, and their retreat after the World War II were due to secularist and humanistic factors: The new science provided the technological capability of traveling to all corners of the globe making this planet truly one world. Similarly, the demand for self-determination, democracy, and human rights has been carried from the salons of Paris and London to Canada, Australia, India, Zimbabwe, and other far corners of the earth. Today the entire world appreciates the power of the scientific revolution and the fruits of industry and technology. But the scientific revolution has languished, and there is a need to develop it further. In particular, we need to challenge those religious institutions that have impeded the full development of the humanist outlook and morality. For it is not enough to use science and technology without appreciating the methods of rational inquiry and without transforming our view of the universe and of our moral and social values. In particular, we need a reappraisal of values to accommodate the new world of scientific and technological discovery. That is, I believe, the primary imperative of the twenty-first century: we need a new global and cosmic humanism that expresses a revolutionary approach to values. We must be willing to reconstruct the values of humankind, overcoming the parochial racial, ethnic, nationalistic, and religious prejudices of the past. We need a new moral philosophy, appropriate to the emerging challenges of the future, with daring new visions.

But if these goals are to be fulfilled, I submit that there are two further aspects of the humanist agenda that must be implemented. First, there needs to be vigorous criticism of the false religious mythologies and theologies of today. This means that humanism needs again to be authentically *radical* in its approach. We need to embark upon sustained criticism of all forms of fundamentalist theological nonsense, especially insofar as it seeks to block the world of the future. There appears to be an ingrained reluctance among some humanists to do so. It is considered to be impolite, in bad taste, or excessively revolutionary. Many humanists make common cause with liberal religionists, especially in defending the democratic values that we share, and do not wish to alienate them by attacking religious faith. Some even believe that humanism is, or should be religious and should ape religions by organizing nontheistic chapters, societies, churches, or temples.

Now I can appreciate their strategies, but I dissent from them if it means that the humanists must mute their strong critiques of the Bible, the Koran, the Book of Mormon, and other so-called sacred documents. For what is ignored by this passive policy is the fact that most religious movements are themselves expansionist and constantly seek to win the minds of men and women by universalist appeals based upon unexamined theological premises. In *their* missionary efforts *they* attack those who differ with them, and they make no apologies for doing so. Their chief enemies when they are not fighting one another, are humanism, unbelief, atheism, and skepticism, and they are never reluctant to point out our failings. I think we must do the same. Many humanists, rationalists, and secularists think that the victory has been won, and that no one any longer takes seriously questions concerning the existence of God or the revelatory claims of the Bible and the Koran. How wrong they are. It should be apparent that every generation needs to keep alive the faculty of criticism, including the debunking of theological pretensions. The victories of the past can never be secured in the present or the future unless we are constantly aware of the issues at stake. In my judgment, the world humanist movement needs to embark anew on aggressive criticism of fundamentalist and conservative religious claims. We must keep alive the spirit of biblical criticism, whose rich tradition has largely been lost to so many of our generation. I should point out that in many countries the things that we care about most are often threatened because of unexamined theological prejudices. I have in mind liberty of thought; moral freedom; the right to privacy, abortion, and euthanasia; and the desire to end discrimination and to achieve peace and social justice.

Thus humanism is and should be identified with non-theism, atheism, and agnosticism—or, as I prefer to call it, "skepticism." It should not be dogmatic or fanatic in its opposition, but carefully responsible, yet willing to voice criticism of the many outrageous and unproven claims of theism. And these critiques ought to be offered with courage and conviction and without fear or timidity, even though we may risk condemnation by the religious establishments. I can think of nothing more important in the third world today than this defense of critical skepticism, including science and humanism in regard to the illusions of the orthodox systems of religious belief. Humanism must be on the cutting edge of a new tomorrow, and we need to enlist the best scientific and scholarly minds in this cause.

But if we are to achieve a humanistic world, we must develop anew our creative imagination. We need to create inspiring new moral and aesthetic equivalents of the transcendental temptation. If we are to sublimate this powerful urge in the human breast, we need to provide constructive alternatives. With the near collapse today of revolutionary utopian visions, humanists have been reluctant to dream of new frontiers for humankind to conquer. But how will we convince others of the grandeur and power of the humanist agenda if we do not dare to dream of possible futures that can captivate and fascinate humanity. Unfortunately, humanism is now considered to be a boring rehash of yesterday's clichés; it is often the rearguard defending a retreating army rather than the avant garde of a new movement with new ideas.

I cannot here fully outline what such a dynamic and positive humanism would entail; for the new humanism of tomorrow should be the cooperative effort of many hands. I will, however, suggest three possible directions that we may take.

1. *Beyond religion.* We need to present the ideal of creating a new civilization that will transcend the need for the religions of the past. We need to show that it is possible to outgrow the religious fixations of the infancy of the race. What will the world of tomorrow be like? What kind of new institutions will we have to create to supplant ancient temples, churches, and mosques? Those of us who are *secular* humanists believe that we have an obligation to create a nonreligious humanism, which nonetheless would give meaning to life and contribute significantly to the enrichment of life for all men and women.

2. *Beyond ethnicity.* We also need to take the lead again, as we did forty or fifty years ago, in defending the ideal of the world community, beyond parochial ethnic, religious, racial, or nationalistic loyalties and frontiers. Although the political and economic difficulties of building such a world are enormous, men and women do not live by bread alone, and it is the moral ideal that must inspire them: that of a *global,* though pluralistic, civilization.

3. *Cosmic humanism.* Perhaps the most exciting aspect of creating a new humanism is the need to transcend the limits of a mentality confined to the planet Earth and to embark upon the building of a humanism appropriate to the space age. In this adventure, we will no doubt compete with tradi-

tional religions, which have always talked about the "unseen world" of the "heavenly bodies," but which reduce this in the last analysis to anthropocentric dimensions of faith and mystery. I am not betraying humanism in saying that we need to look beyond the earth. The human species has already begun space exploration and travel. By using the rigorous methods of science and technology, we have for the first time been able to view Mars, Jupiter, Saturn, Neptune, Uranus, and the comet Halley up close. Many of the leaders of the world humanist movement are deeply involved as scientists in charting the frontiers of space and speculating about it (Carl Sagan, Isaac Asimov, Francis Crick, Fred Hoyle, et al.). We need to soar with them and imagine a new future in which we may be able to colonize outer space: first our own solar system and then beyond it. Perhaps we may even encounter extraterrestrial civilizations. What a great and daring challenge for Promethean humanism. Prometheus, you will recall, stole fire and the arts of science and civilization from the gods and bequeathed them to mankind. Is it not our task to explore the heavenly domain of the mythological gods themselves? What an exciting challenge awaits the humanism of the future as we depart from our earthly terrain and soar into the cosmos.

What should be patently clear is that the human family lives together on the planet Earth and that the ancient myths and divisive theologies invented by the speculative imagination of the past will no longer suffice in the future. We need to make sense out of the universe in which we live. But we can do so only by testing our hypotheses and theories by the rigorous methods of science. We can only do so if we recognize that the high priests of the past are inadequate to the task. It is not the theologians or mystics who will point the way, but the astrophysicists and astronomers. We need to embark together on the task of building a new and relevant global and cosmic humanism that will be truly appropriate to the great exploratory adventures of the twenty-first century that await us.

NOTES

1. Quoted in "Where in the World is the Church Growing," by Sharon E. Mumper, *Christianity Today,* July 11, 1986.
2. Ibid.
3. Ibid.
4. An editorial in the August 8, 1986, issue of *Christianity Today* (p. 14) applauds this development. "The Christian mission to people in other cultures has undergone radical changes in the last century. C. T. Studd was one of the famous 'Cambridge Seven' who went to China in the 1880s with the China Inland Mission. He reported: 'For five years we never went outside our doors without a volley of curses from our neighbors.' H. J. Kane also cites nineteenth-century missionaries in an undocumented quotation of one of the Chinese *literati:* 'We would sooner go to hell with our Confucius than go to heaven with your Jesus.' He then adds: 'These quotations point up a major contrast between the 19th and 20th centuries. In the 19th century, thanks to our colonial system, the doors to the Third World were wide open—politically; but the hearts of the people were closed against the gospel.' . . .

"But today, political realities have all but reversed themselves. Newly independent Third World governments have broken away from political imperialism and are seeking to complete their independence by cutting off what they deem cultural imperialism. It is becoming increasingly difficult to get into some countries, and other countries are closed to the Christian missionary. But if one can only get in, he or she often finds the hearts of the people wide open.

"George Gallup, Jr., argues that there is abroad in the world an almost universal hunger for spiritual reality. Never have the masses in Africa and Asia been so open to claims of Christ. And this includes people in all walks of life. As missions historian George Peters sees it: 'This is indeed the day of salvation as far as the Third World is concerned.' "

5. Edward O. Wilson, *Sociobiology: The New Synthesis* (Cambridge: Harvard University Press, 1975).

6. For an in-depth discussion of this thesis see my book. *The Transcendental Temptation* (Buffalo, N.Y.: Prometheus Books, 1986).

The Threat of Neo-Fundamentalism

Gerald A. Larue

Fundamentalism began in response to questions concerning biblical authority that developed out of modern science and higher and lower criticism of the Bible. For example, traditional views of creationism were challenged both by geology and by biblical research. Higher criticism questioned the assumption that the Bible—and in America in particular, the King James Version—was the divinely inspired word of God delivered and preserved without error. It was demonstrated that the Bible had many human authors and these writers did not always agree with one another. Even the Torah, ascribed by pious Jews and Christians to Moses, was shown to be a composite work that underwent editing and re-editing between the tenth and fifth centuries Before the Common Era (B.C.E).

The relationship between the synoptic Gospels (Matthew, Mark, and Luke) was exposed, demonstrating that the gospel writers used other sources and that each was not the unique memory of a single person who may have known Jesus. Matthew and Luke used Mark plus a collection of sayings attributed to Jesus, which scholars called *Quelle* (Q), meaning "source." Each added unique materials from his own sources. Gospel writers had angles of vision or differing points of view. They wrote for different audiences. Sayings attributed to Jesus were given different settings by the gospel writers. These and other similar observations raised serious questions about Jesus' historicity and about which sayings might be considered authentic and which were the product of the early church, and so on. The accepted image of Jesus was threatened. It was as if one peeled an onion and as layer after layer of accumulated folklore and theological fiction was removed, the historical Jesus was reduced to a small kernal devoid of form or character.

Lower criticism traced the manuscript history of the Bible. Scribal errors were plentiful because the copyists were human. Older and better manuscripts challenged some translations in the King James Version.

The Bible had not been preserved and translated in its purity. It was made up of a collection of writings that had been composed and edited over a 1200 year period extending from the tenth century B.C.E. to the second century of the Common Era (C.E.). Critical examination gave clues to the time and place of writing of the various parts and revealed the attitudes and biases of composers and editors. Moreover, the copyists had provided translators with a wide variety of manuscript variations.

These findings were not the product of destructive efforts by atheists or enemies of the faith. They were the result of serious research by scholars who were believers. Consequently, these new findings became part of the seminary programs in mainline denominations. Newly trained clergy were ready to share these findings with their congregations. They did not always receive a welcome.

The Divinity School of the University of Chicago produced excellent, readable pamphlets written by eminent scholars who provided the latest and best information concerning biblical scholarship. The Reverend Harry Emerson Fosdick utilized some of the findings of modern biblical research.

Through his writings and his radio preaching, he reached an international audience from his New York pulpit. Modern scholarship was reaching the masses through mainline churches.

On the other hand, the fundamentalists were reacting. Those holding to biblical infallibility stated the five fundamentals of their position at the Niagara Conference in 1895. According to Williston Walker, they were "the inerrancy of Scripture, the deity of Jesus, the virgin birth, the substitutionary atonement, and the physical resurrection and bodily return of Christ."[1] Fundamentalist presses produced and gave away millions of free pamphlets proclaiming their interpretation of biblical "truth." The Bible tract movement had begun about 1900 with contributions written by eminent evangelicals including James B. Orr, B. B. Warfield, H. C. G. Moule and G. Campbell Morgan. As Reverend Fosdick took to the airwaves, so did the fundamentalists.

Within the mainline churches there was reaction against "modernism" and "higher criticism." Splits occurred in denominations as members asked: "If the claims of modern biblical scholarship are taken seriously, what happens to the authority of the Bible and to the teachings ascribed to Jesus, or to Jesus' identity as Lord and Savior?" and "Is modern scholarship destroying the Bible?"

Few liberal scholars were ready to let their scholarship lead them to the obvious conclusion that the Bible was nothing more than the expressed beliefs of Jews and Christians who lived two to three thousand years ago, possessing no more authority than any other ancient literature. Many made what was called "the leap of faith," by which they separated their research from their devotional life and simply accepted "on faith" the reality of God, the primacy of Jesus, and the sayings attributed to them as valid for life and living.

Many of the earlier fundamentalists were not trained in

biblical and semitic languages and literature. They were no match for their liberal opponents. Now neo-fundamentalism insisted on the best higher education for their seminary instructors and for their preachers. Neo-fundamentalist scholars were trained in biblical languages and Near Eastern history in first-rate universities, including Harvard and Yale. Insofar as it was possible, they avoided confrontational classes. They read the findings of critical scholarship and then sought ways to refute those claims. Indeed, some began to argue that they were the ones dealing with facts while liberal scholars were missing or ignoring the evidence. Their voices became louder as their influence increased through the work of devoted followers, radio and television ministries, door-to-door evangelism, and so on.

Meanwhile, liberal biblical scholarship continued to develop analytical approaches to the Bible. To the well-established historical-critical method of inquiry there was added form criticism, *tendenz* criticism, redaction criticism, structural exegesis, and so on. Each of these approaches was developed within the context of the church by scholars who professed a belief in God, as revealed in the Bible, and in Jesus as Messiah. Some concluded that Jesus had been a mild-mannered Jew who preached the fatherhood of God and the brotherhood of man until he ran into difficulty with some of his countrymen and the Roman authorities.

Mainline preachers were on the firing line. Trained in biblical criticism, when they attempted to share their findings with their congregations they faced criticism and the development of splinter movements within the denomination. I can recall visiting a community where one church bore the label, First Presbyterian Church, another The Bible Presbyterian Church, another The True Presbyterian Church, and still another The Only True Presbyterian Church. The "mother church," so to speak, had been the first church; the others were separatist organizations. Some liberal clergy borrowed notions from the neo-fundamentalists. The Bible, they claimed, was given by inspiration to the original writers and therefore the "autographs," which are of course not available to us, were without error. Subsequent copyists introduced errors. Others suggested that the inspiration was valid but inasmuch as God was working through fallible human beings, errors occurred. These answers simply raised another question: "If God was so concerned about getting his divine word to humans, why was he not equally concerned about its transmission, preservation, and translation?" One preacher told me of a personal compromise of scholarship and preaching that he used so as to maintain his inner integrity: "When I speak of the historical Jesus I use the word 'Jesus,' and when I refer to the theological Christ as developed in the New Testament and the church's theology, I use the term 'Christ.' " When I asked if he shared this information with his congregation, he said he did not, because it would only serve to divide his church. He felt he was maintaining his personal scholarly integrity while meeting his responsibilities as a preacher to his flock.

Fundamentalists continued to attack modern scholarship as the enemy of the faith and the destroyer of God-given biblical truth. Modernism accepted Darwinian and evolutionary concepts that undermined biblical creationism. Neo-fundamentalists sought to develop a biblical science that would provide a different interpretation of the findings of geology, astronomy, and similar sciences to accommodate the creation myths. Their scholars read archeological reports and interpreted them in ways that supported their beliefs. Their writers wrote volumes interpreting research in ways that supported biblical inerrancy. Neo-fundamentalism was moving forward, declaring itself prepared to respond with traditional answers in new format for some of life's questions.

Fundamentalism surged during the Great Depression. Their preachers taught that as American liberalism had abandoned the God of the Bible, the God of the Bible had abandoned America. The way to economic recovery was through a return to the Bible. It was a time for true believers to speak out. In Alberta, Canada, the Social Credit movement had its origins in a fundamentalist Baptist church. William Aberhart, who was principal of Crescent Heights High School during the week and a powerful radio evangelist on weekends, informed one class of graduating students that he was weary of watching promising students leave the portals of the school to enter a society that had no place for them. He proposed to make economic changes to improve that situation. His radio pulpit provided him with a powerful tool to reach the public. His congregation, composed of dedicated, hard-working followers, gave of themselves to support him. His preaching, which appealed to biblical authority, evoked a response in the basically conservative Albertans, and combined with his deep concern for human welfare, made it possible for him to become the first Social Credit Premier of the province. Religion and politics were being wedded here and elsewhere in American thought.

During the postwar period, fundamentalism began a renewed outreach. Some clergy announced that the world had entered into "the last days" and God was about to fulfill biblical prophecies about the end of time. It did not seem to matter that these predictions had proved to be wrong over and over again in past centuries,[2] they still attracted followers. Others emphasized the Bible as a guide to successful living, to good family life, to meaningful existence. Slogans such as "families that pray together, stay together" implied that the rising divorce rate could be stemmed through family worship. Of course such teachings were demonstrably wrong, as the divorce rate among church-going families roughly paralleled that of non-church families. Other groups focused on faith-healing, arguing that the only requirement for healing human ailments was faith in the power of God and the name of Jesus. Tent ministries like that of Oral Roberts became popular. Bily Graham's campaigns, stressing the need for conversion and faith in Jesus as savior, were held in large population centers. In each instance the programs were carefully orchestrated. The Billy Graham crusade employed organizers who met with church leaders in the large cities more than a year before the campaign began. Each church promised so many busloads of worshippers and so many choir members so that the auditoriums were guaranteed to be 95 percent filled with church people—the already converted— leaving only 5 percent of the seating space for those who might be unaffiliated. Every step of the program was carefully planned so that when someone rose to answer the altar call, there was a faith-guide to walk down the aisle with him or her. Sentimental music, particularly the hymn "Just as I am," without one plea . . ." was sung over and over again with its sacharine conclusion, "O Lamb of God, I come, I come," and the audience was moved to come forward for prayer and salvation. Most of those who responded were already Christians who were simply reaffirming their faith. The cards filled out by respondents were distributed to those ministers who had cooperated in the campaign in the hope that new church members would be found. In most cases the results were disappointing.

Oral Roberts centered his message on healing, a phenomenon largely ignored in most Christian churches. His claims to miraculous cures made local hospitals appear inadequate, unless one followed upon the "healed." But the neo-fundamentalist emphasis on faith-healing and the salvation preaching of Billy Graham and others had an impact not only on those who attended the meetings but on radio and television listeners and viewers as well.

Within mainline churches the issue of biblical scholarship
tended to be handled with caution. For example, I was invited
to give a series of public lectures on biblical scholarship at
a local college traditionally affiliated with a conservative, but
not fundamentalist religious tradition. The minister of the
local Methodist church, who has been in some of the same
classes on Bible that I had attended at Pacific School of
Religion in Berkeley, urged his congregation to attend. I asked
him why, since he could provide them with similar information.
He responded: "They will listen to you and either accept or
reject what is said. If I should give the same material there
would be a reaction that would split the church and I am
not about to do that!"

Some clergy became interested in the theologies of Karl
Barth and Emil Brunner and stressed neo-orthodoxy. Others
experimented with dialectical theology, Kierkegaardianism,
or existential theology. New translations of the Bible opened
the door to an emphasis on biblical religion. When the Revised
Standard Version, produced by scholars under the aegis of
the National Council of Churches, appeared in 1952, a veri-
table storm of protest developed. Fundamentalists called it
the "Communist Bible,"[3] challenged the religious commitment
of the translators, and produced hundreds of pamphlets and
preached thousands of sermons opposing it.[4] With the royalties
received from Thomas Nelson and Sons, and with special
money provided by the publisher, a special Committee for
the Use and Understanding of the Bible was set up. Meetings
of clergy were held in hamlets, towns, and cities in which
biblical scholars helped to develop community programs
centered on biblical history, the history of translations,
archaeological exhibits related to the Bible, and so on. The
fundamentalists, through pamphlets and radio preaching
continued to attack, focusing on particular passages and

especially on some verses that were put in italicized footnotes to indicate that the verses were not found in the earliest and best manuscripts and were to be reckoned as late additions made by devout Christians. The two passages were specifically attacked: Mark 16:9–19 and John 7:53–8:11. Some footnotes were dropped and a few terms were changed. For example, a footnote at Matthew 1:16, based on the text of The Sinaitic Syriac version, that dealt with Jesus' geneology read, "Jacob begot Joseph. And Joseph, to whom was betrothed Virgin Mary, begot Jesus who is called the Christ." Despite the fact that this particular reading, in the words of Sherman E. Johnson, "fits better with the original purpose of the geneology," it was dropped from the footnotes.[5] Truly, the fundamentalists had a cause célèbre on which to attack modernism.

In recent years the fundamentalist movement has enjoyed a new birth through the extended use of radio and television. Faith-healing, which the Committee for the Scientific Examination of Religion has, in some cases, exposed as deliberately deceptive and void of the claims made by certain televangelists, continues to attract desperate but unwary ailing persons and their families. The roots of faith-healing are biblical, and claims of miraculous cures have been made throughout the centuries. Now, however, with media hype, the claims have become more and more exaggerated, and only scientific examination can reveal that the claims are unfounded. The latest enemy of fundamentalism has become the humanist movement. In the past the devil was associated with the papacy or with modernism. Now the devil is in charge of the humanist movement, which is the clear enemy of fundamentalism. Because our modern public schools are concerned with providing students with the best scientific education, there has been incorporated within their science textbooks scientific findings concerning the evolution of the solar system, the earth, and its inhabitants. The findings do not coincide with biblical concepts that reflect the way human beings thought several thousand years ago. Hence the neo-fundamentalists pit the Bible against modern science, and because humanism accepts the best scientific findings, it has by some queer twist of logic, become the enemy. Humanistic ethics stress freedom, emphasize the rights of minorities and women, accept homosexuals as people, challenge the use of physical force in educating the young, and so on. This ethical stance is recognized as a denial of biblical ethics, which support opposite points of view.

Within neo-fundamentalism the new emphasis on apocalypticism reflects the present-day loss of faith in our human ability to come to terms with one another and to solve our problems peacefully. Only God can resolve modern tensions by bringing all existence to an end, by rewarding the true fundamentalists for their faith, and by punishing others—in particular humanists—for their lack of faith.[6]

One of the more recent trends in the United States is the entry of avowed fundamentalists into the political arena. Most presidential candidates have admitted publicly their association with some religious body. It was unusual for a Roman Catholic, John F. Kennedy, to win the highest office. It was also unusual for a fundamentalist like Jimmy Carter to become president. Both of these men kept their religious beliefs in very low key and were able to avoid the criticism that they were trying to press their own beliefs into the government and hence into public life. This has not been so with Ronald Reagan, who has not hidden his close association with right-wing neo-fundamentalists and who has used the power of his office to try to influence legislation that is in accord with ultra-conservative theology. For example, in his stance on abortion, his comments echo those of the ultra-right fundamentalists. He has also expressed his concerns for the divine end-of-time in language that again echoes the beliefs of the biblicists. His public stance can only serve to encourage others who embrace a more extreme fundamentalist position to decide to run for public office. In President Reagan's efforts to pack the Supreme Court with appointees who agree with his ultra-conservative beliefs, his influence may affect the well-being of unborn millions.

Neo-fundamentalism could become a world threat because what happens in America affects the rest of the world. If Islamic neo-fundamentalism in Iran can affect the world in greater or lesser degree, one can only imagine the impact of Christian neo-fundamentalism endorsed by the leadership of the most powerful nation in the world.

What is equally insidious are the efforts being made in America to compel modern schools to teach courses in what is called "Creation Science," which is, in reality, the continuing effort to deny the findings of modern science and to place biblical creationism on a level equal to, if not superior to, evolution. Certain groups have been influential in causing textbook writers to modify and water down comments relating to evolution. The presence in libraries of the best science reference books has been questioned. Indeed librarians have been confronted by right-wing groups objecting to the inclusion of certain literary classics and books on art as well as volumes relating to science in public school collections.

Prime-time programs aired on the media have been criticized, and there are groups of fundamentalists who are calling for the portrayal of families engaged in prayer: pronouncing "grace" at meals or attending church. Others have denounced the elimination of programs that portray the clergy or religion in an unfavorable light, even when such programs may be based on real-life situations.

The pressure is relentless. Defeat in one situation only seems to encourage efforts in another, while victory in any given set of circumstances becomes a call to challenge elsewhere. Even as the neo-fundamentalists continue to try to force their biblical concepts on the general public, those committed to the transmission of the best and finest in education must be unrelenting in their resistance to these pressures. It would seem that the best way to defeat the ultra-right-wing efforts is to continue to share publicly the best information that we possess concerning our world, the basis upon which our conclusions are reached, and the developing ethic that raises our human condition somewhat closer to the highest dreams that humans have entertained throughout our long, long history—dreams that move far beyond the narrow and restrictive concepts of the Bible.

NOTES

1. Williston Walker, *A History of the Christian Church* (New York: Scribners, 1959), p. 517.

2. Gerald A. Larue, "Dimensions of Apocalyptic Thinking," *Free Inquiry* 4, no. 3 (1984): 39–41.

3. The fact that it was issued with a red cover was also stated as evidence of its Communist leanings! Other derogatory labels included "The Devil's Masterpiece," "Modernism's Unholy Bible," etc.

4. Cf. Gerald A. Larue, "Another Chapter in the History of Bible Translation," *The Journal of Bible and Religion* 31, no. 4 (1963): 301–310.

5. Sherman E. Johnson, "Introduction and Exegesis: Matthew," *The Interpreter's Bible,* New York, 1951, Vol. 7, p. 253.

6. See *Free Inquiry* 4, no. 3, (1984), and the "Special Feature" titled: "Armageddon: Are We Living in the Last Days?"

The Return to Islamic Fundamentalism

Vern L. Bullough

During periods of rapid change, when challenges to the old ways of doing things seem to be undermining traditional values, fundamentalism in its various guises has great appeal. It offers simple answers to complex problems and allows the believer to see everything in black and white and to ignore all the shades in between.

When these rapid changes are taking place in areas of the world that during much of the nineteenth and twentieth centuries were dominated by Western powers, fundamentalism inevitably takes on an anti-Western guise, looking for its strength in sources of tradition within that society. Often the embodiment of traditional values are religious institutions, as they are in the Islamic world, and then religion becomes the bulwark of fundamentalism.

Islam has some particular features as a religion that supply the ingredients for a particularly virulent form of fundamentalism. To explain the existence of these ingredients, some knowledge of history is important. Islam first appeared not in a powerful state as did Christianity, but among one of the tribal groups contesting power in the Arabian peninsula. It soon proved to be the unifying power for the Arabs who then, under the banner of Islam, expanded rapidly. Islam and the state were the same, and Islam never had a Jesus

or a St. Augustine who defined the realm of the spiritual
as different from that of the secular. Islam, in fact, lacks
a separation between the temporal and spiritual. Both are
regarded as representing two aspects of the same essence.
Every human action includes its religious or motivational as
well as its mundane causes and effects. Though Islamic law
and government are in one sense temporal, since they control
human behavior of all kinds, the source and objectives are
spiritual. Sir Mohammed Iqbal summed it up:

> In Islam it is the same reality which appears as Church
> looked at from one point of view and State from another.
> It is not true to say that Church and State are two sides
> or facets of the same thing. Islam is a single unanalyzable
> reality which is one or the other as your point of view
> varies.[1]

This view has had disastrous intellectual and social consequences upon Islamic countries and peoples in the past, and
it makes the dangers of Islamic fundamentalism loom much
larger upon the world scene than the rise of fundamentalist-
evangelical Christianity in such countries as the United States.

By the nature of its origins, Islam has always emphasized
the formation of the *Umma,* a community of believers who
accepted the revelations of the prophet Muhammed. *Umma*
is a nation bound neither by physical nor psychological
attributes nor by cultural affinities. Instead, almost from the
beginning the *Umma* has been a multi-racial and multi-ethnic
community united by belief. This belief transcends family,
clan, and tribe, and results in the formation of a larger community, i.e., those who have a belief in Islam.[2] Though the
Umma at first united only rival Arab tribes, committing them
to the common goal of a revealed religion, it soon spread
to encompass non-Arab territories and peoples. As these were
incorporated, *Umma* moved from a concept of Arab

ethnocentrism, if it ever was so limited, to a universal one. Originally a purely religious entity, it also became a cultural entity fostering spiritual development, internal continuity, and a sense of cohesion.[3]

The initial result was a golden intellectual age for Islam, an age to which the Western world owes an almost incalculable debt. The Muslim expansion served as one of the great cultural transmitters of history, picking up Greek philosophical and scientific concepts, and adding to these ideas garnered from the Middle East and India, as well as China, making these concepts their own, and then giving them back to Europe in modified form. The works of Aristotle, of Hippocrates, of Galen, and especially the Greek mathematicians and scientists were lost to Western Europe except through simplified Latin condensations in the early Middle Ages (this was not true of Plato). Historians have traced the recovery of this corpus of knowledge through an Islamic transmission belt that began with translations of many of these works by Nestorian Christians into Syriac, and from Syriac to Arabic. These Arab translations, commentators and a new basic corpus of Islamic learning reached the West originally through contacts between Muslims and Christians in Spain and in southern Italy. Often the transmission belt included a translation from Arabic to Hebrew to Latin, although many also went directly from Arabic to Latin. The Islamic culture seemed to gather in, to absorb, and expand upon ideas, concepts, and techniques from all parts of Asia, Europe, and Africa. In transmitting these to Europe, Islamic intellectuals left their imprint on Western development. Hunayn ibn Ishaq, together with his son and nephew, translated most of the important Greek scientific writings into Arabic in the ninth century, and the work he began was built upon by individuals such as Rhazes, a person who wrote more than 200 works, Issac Judaeus, an Egyptian Jew, and Avicenna, the author of the great *Canon* of Medicine. There was Al Kindi, who broke new ground in optics, al Khwarizmi and Omar Khayyam, both mathematicians, the latter the founder of analytical geometry. The Arabs picked up the Hindu numeral system, particularly the zero, developed Algebra, and passed both on to change the nature of thinking in the West. Averroes, the Spanish Muslim, developed the kind of logical questions which Christians such as Albertus Magnus and Thomas Aquinas later spent their lives in trying to answer. Words such as alcohol, algebra, cipher, alchemy, aluminum, and hundreds of others came from the Arabic. In fact there originally were many more Arabic terms in Western science, but in the sixteenth century there was a deliberate attempt to eliminate them by reemphasizing Greek or Latin base words as the source of scientific terms. Like the Christians who succeeded them, the Islamic writers worked within the limits of their religion, that is, they were mainly concerned with the conflict between revelation and reason and argued that revelation was compatible with reason. Human laws, devised by reason, were the function of scientists and philosophers to determine but only as they applied to revelation. These Islamic writers tried to do for Islam what Aquinas later tried to do to Christianity, make it logically consistent. Just as Aquinas Christianized Aristotle, they Islamicized him.[4]

This tremendous Islamic intellectual expansion and dialogue came to a halt at the end of the eleventh century as political and economic disaster threatened the heartland of Islam from Christian crusaders to the Golden Horde to the Mongols to the Turks. Though many of the conquerors of the Arab heartlands ultimately converted to Islam, and Islam continued to expand in Africa south of the Sahara and into such areas as Indonesia, the golden age of Islam declined rather drastically. A major reason for this is that as Islamic rulers came under attack and ultimate defeat, many within Islam argued that it was because Muslims had become much too worldly, too secular, and that in the process they had strayed from the *Umma*. One result was what has been called a return to fundamentalism, which entailed a denial of the validity of philosophical speculation and a more rigid adherence to the laws of the Koran and the legal tradition.

Defeated or threatened externally, many in the Islamic world also turned inward, to asceticism and mysticism, the most popular form of which was Sufism.[5] Sufis taught that ultimate happiness was the unification of oneself with the Absolute and the Infinite, that which alone is beyond all limitation and is absolutely free. The result was a contempt for the things of this earth, an emphasis upon examination of the soul, an effort to achieve the absorption of one's personality in the one real divine existence.[6]

The ultimate goal of the Sufi was the dissolution of the individual into the sole reality of divine existence, and the key to this was love. Through the love of God, the soul could dissolve its separateness into the truth of and unity with an all-encompassing divine being. To achieve this required concentration on improving one's self for unity with the universe and the avoidance of involvement with the changing worldly order. It resulted in a downplaying of intellectual tradition and a kind of fundamentalism and an acceptance of authority figures since ultimately only the unity with God mattered.

Sufism was other worldly, but for those Muslims interested in the world, there was a different kind of intellectual retreat, namely, following the words and directions of the *Ulama*, religious leaders who were the interpreters of Islamic law and in theory the moral directors of the Islamic rulers. Under the Ottoman Empire (fifteenth to the nineteenth century), the Ulamas were subordinated to the military and political powers of the Ottoman rulers. This power was maintained by a professional army, by the legal system, and by the abilities of the sultan to select from the *Ulama* a *Mufti,* a leader to interpret Islamic law and obligations to the community. Thus adherence to the rule of the sultan was a religious as well as civil obligation, and again a kind of nonintellectual fundamentalism dominated.

By the end of the eighteenth century, Turkish power found itself on the defensive, retreating against the expansion of Russia to the north and east and against Austria to the north and west, as well as the penetration of the French and English into the Islamic heartlands in the Middle Ease, India, and later in Africa. In order to protect his power, the sultan attempted to Westernize the bureaucracy and the army, and within limits, to liberalize. This was not particularly successful and, in fact, again encouraged religious leaders to blame the growing weakness of Islamic society on loss of belief and on corrupt practices. In many areas of the Islamic world, the response was a return to fundamentalism, a renewed dedication to Islam as occurred with the rise of the Wahhabi sect in the mid-eighteenth century. This group, which appeared first in central Arabia, advocated a return to puritanical Islam and the removal of all the divisive factors of urban life.

The success of such movements made it difficult for would-be secular reformers of Islamic society. They had to demonstrate that their principles were no less advanced than those of Europe, but in order to sell themselves to their fellow Muslims, they also had to indicate that they were no less Islamic than those of the established conservative tradition. These dual requirements tended to mitigate against systematic rigorous thought but instead encouraged superficial slogans and angry polemics. Among those most capable of breaking out of the fundamentalist stranglehold, it resulted in a premium being put on ingenuity and nimble equivocation rather than on sustained thought. Unlike the medieval Muslim intellectuals who could assert their consciences in the face of established tradition, Muslim thinkers now had the more difficult task of finding their consciences in the midst of two contrasting traditions, or if we take into account the Soviet revolution, in the midst of three, Islamic-Western-Marxian.

The issue was further complicated by the growing presence of westerners in such areas as Syria, Algeria, Egypt, India, and (to a lesser extent) elsewhere. In many areas those best able to articulate the new Western ideas were indigenous Christians or Jews, and often the colonial powers adopted a policy of advancing these "non-believers" over their Islamic compatriots. Thus, as Islamic fundamentalism grew stronger, it often made scapegoats of these Christians and Jews, who, under the Ottoman *Milli* system had been able to freely practice their religion and have their personal and familial disputes judged by their own religious leaders and traditions.

The British relied upon the Coptic Christians in Egypt, the French supported the Marionite and other Christian communities in what came to be Lebanon, and splinter groups such as the Druse also found support among the Western powers. American missionaries established Christian schools in Turkey, Lebanon, Egypt, and elsewhere; some of these developed into colleges establishing a foothold for Western-style education. Even the Universities of Cairo, Ain Shams, and Alexandria in Egypt were heavily influenced by English or French Christian models. This tended to complicate the relationship of Islam with Western secular learning since it was often seen as being anti-Islamic.

In areas such as Egypt, which had a large Jewish community—and in many ways the most Westernized intellectual group—Jews also contributed in important ways to the intellectual tradition, and perhaps in the long run might have been able to be a more effective bridge between traditional Islam and the demands of the modern world. But the creation of modern Israel made them even more suspect as sources of knowledge than their Christian counterparts.

If Islam passively smouldered at the growth of Westernized intellectual traditions among such groups as Christians and Jews, they were hostile to those Muslims who seemed to abandon Islamic tradition for any form of Western ideology. This is illustrated by the Islamic reaction to Bahaism in Islamic areas. Originally an Islamic sect, Bahai emerged from Persian Shiism in the nineteenth century. Based upon the teachings of the prophet Sayyid Ali Muhammed, who called himself Bab (the gateway), the movement coalesced under Baha-ullah after the execution of Sayyid in 1850. It was a syncretic movement emphasizing pacificism and humanitarianism that found most of its adherents outside the Islamic world. In fact the hostility directed toward Bahai disciples and believers during the recent Iranian revolution indicates just how much hostility toward "Islamic heretics" exists among Islamic fundamentalists.

Complicating the effort of would-be reformers was the pressure of time. This is most evident in the case of Muhammad Abduh (d. 1905), the Egyptian reformer who held the view that if Islamic beliefs and attitudes were not reformed in time, they would soon erode at a rapid pace, leaving a moral vacuum in their place. But how does one reform? Rashid Rida, who followed Abduh, turned to restating the classics of the Islamic age in modern dress, and in the process gave them radically different meanings more suited to the modern world. This resulted in frequent contradictions since the resulting product is both radical and conservative. Rashid, for example, ended up being a radical in some of his theoretical positions, conservative in building up the past, and reactionary in his conclusions.[7]

The very extent of the challenge of the West to traditional Islamic concepts left the intellectuals in these countries with few options to follow. They could either "sell" out to the

West and adopt or promulgate such "foreign" ideas as Marxism in its various guises, or turn to capitalism, no matter how we define it, or to any other Western *ism*, in which case they would find themselves alienated from their Islamic culture and from their people. Alternatively they could try to reinterpret Islam to meet the current demands of the world. Regardless of their motive in doing the latter, by simply emphasizing the importance of Islam, the initial result would be Islamic fundamentalism since by strengthening Islam they would set off a fundamentalist reaction among people who would feel threatened by forces they could not control.

Inevitably both fundamentalists and modernists in Islamic thought seemed to have emphasized a return to Islam. This can be illustrated briefly by the career of four major Islamic thinkers of this century, two who were avowedly fundamentalists and two who consider themselves reformers. Probably the most influential figures of the return to Islamic fundamentals have been Sayyid Qutb (1906–1966) of the Muslim Brotherhood and Mawlana Abu al-Alla Mawdudi (1903–1979) of the Islamic Association. Both were prodigious writers whose books were translated and circulated widely throughout the Islamic world. After flirting with Western Ideology, both men came to believe that "alien" models were incapable of providing the sense of identity and moral purpose that the Islamic world needed, and so they became convinced that only a return to Islamic fundamentals would provide the answer. Muhammed Iqbal (1875-1938) and Ali Shariati (1933-1977), the "reformers," emphasized renovation rather than restoration or replication, but they, too, based their assumptions upon Islamic tradition. Iqbal wanted a new synthesis of Western and Islamic science to provide a bridge between tradition and modernity. Shariati, strongly influenced by Iqbal, sought a more revolutionary Islam distinct from what he called the clerical domination of the immediate past.

Rejecting both uncritical imitation of the West (Westoxifi-
cation) and traditional religious leadership, he became an
ideologue and an early hero of the Iranian revolution.[8]

Each deserves brief examination. Qutb, for example, held
that Islam possessed the necessary capabilities for solving the
basic problems of the world. True Islam would be the source
of a comprehensive social justice, the means of restoring justice
in government, giving economic opportunities, and would free
Muslims from subservience to the West. The Egyptian revolution of 1952, which brought Gamal Abdul Nasser to power,
brought enthusiastic support from the Muslim Brotherhood,
to which Qutb belonged. In fact, upon assuming power, the
Egyptian military officers sent for him and during the first
six months of the new revolutionary regime he functioned
as a consultant, voting on matters of policy with the officers
and trying to influence their plans for the country. He
ultimately left because they refused to institute an Islamic
state and to assign the positions of leadership to committed
Muslims from the membership of the Muslim Brotherhood.
When the Muslim Brotherhood later went into full-scale opposition to Nasser and the "secularization" of Egypt, Qutb, as
one of the leaders, was executed in Cairo in 1966. This did
not end the power of the Brotherhood, which is still influential.[9]

While Qutb was based in Egypt, Mawdudi worked in
Pakistan. Strongly influenced by the British presence in India
(and what later became Pakistan), he initially advised Muslims
not to participate in the political struggle for the independence
of India. Though he was an effective and articulate spokesman
of the need for Islamic politicians to incorporate their Islamic
principles and values into their life and to their schemes for
society, he was not concerned with the practical implemen-
tation of his new Islamic society.[10]

Igbal was more a poet than a philosopher, more a lawyer
than a political thinker, and it was his poetry and his ability

to argue his case for Islam that made him so influential. An Indian, Iqbal studied under Western teachers in India, at Cambridge in England, as well as in Heidelberg and Munich in Germany. Though he admired much that was in the West, he was deeply concerned with what he felt was the crisis in Islamic society, and he felt that the solution to the problem was to be found in building a dynamic and creative Islam. He was opposed to territorial nationalism and in favor of universal Muslim brotherhood, but though in many ways he was a modernist, his emphasis was on Islam and it was the return to Islam that was seized upon by many of his followers.[11]

Ali Shariati, an Iranian, also wanted to base his new society upon the original teachings of Islam, although in his case it was embodied in Shi-ism rather than Sunni Islam. Shariati was a historian who received his doctorate in Paris, but after flirting with Western ideas, he came to believe that the solution to the problems of the Islamic world lay in making the traditions of Islam more pertinent today largely through the use of new terminology and methods. Islamology, or the study of Islam, was to him the means of finding the dynamic ideas within Islam that could be applied to the modern world and offer a true Islamic alternative to Marxism or capitalism or for that matter to the shah of Iran, whom he felt was destructive of Islamic tradition. Shariati's ideas were extremely influential in the early stage of the Iranian revolution, but not all who shouted his slogans had really read or understood what he believed. Shariati died before the shah abdicated.[12]

Though many of the current leaders of the Islamic states are pragmatists, anxious to bring their countries into the modern world, they are conscious of the reviving fundamentalism and are fearful that their countries will be swept up in the movement if they move too rapidly or depart too much from the Islamic tradition. The examples of Libya and Iran are always in their minds. This is true of even the conservative Islamic states, such as Saudi Arabia, that never had a more liberal period and remain under what might be called a modified form of fundamentalist control. Even in Islamic countries that have had a greater tradition of secularism, such as Egypt, Turkey, or Algeria, there is a constant threat of Islamic fundamentalism.

The depth of this threat can easily be demonstrated by what is taking place in the Soviet Union, which in the 1979 census had 43 million people of traditionally Muslim extraction. These areas in the Soviet Union are among the fastest growing segments, and it is estimated that by the year 2000 some 20 percent of the country's total population will be Muslim. It is generally agreed that even those people of Muslim background who do not practice the faith retain Islamic customs. Most are Sunni Muslims, but many of those living in the Azerbaidzhan Republic, across the border from Iran, are Shi-ites. Increasingly Islam has played an important role in the growing national and cultural self-assertion of the predominantly Muslim republics, and in some areas it seems to be establishing itself as a social and religious rival to communism. The 1986 riots that erupted in mid-December in Alma-Ata, capital of Kazahkhstan, are evidence of the powerful nationalist feelings lying below the surface in these Islamic areas. The Soviets are particularly worried about the spread of Iranian Shi-ite fundamentalism across their border. Some indication of this appeared in *Turkmenskaya Iskra*, Turkmenistan's Russian-language newspaper, on 23 November 1986:

> Their frenzied propaganda for Islam conceals their political aims—in effect they wish to liquidate the Socialist system in Central Asia. Their artificial fanning-up of cultural narrowmindedness, political shortsightedness and nationalistic tendencies is a prologue to the disintegration of the USSR.[13]

There has been a rapid growth of unofficial mullahs who perform religious rites, and though the Soviets have moved against them, there is a growing evidence of Islamic fundamentalism and a growing estrangement between Islam and communism, which the Soviet authorities are finding difficult to put down.

In sum, Islamic fundamentalism has strong intellectual roots within Islam, and because of the present historical conditions in Islamic countries, it seems safe to say that we will see a strong trend toward fundamentalism in the immediate forseeable future. Evidence for this is strongly in the Soviet Union, which has emphasized secularism for seventy years. It seems clear that when even reformist ideas result in an emphasis on Islamic fundamentalism, it is a problem that will not easily resolve itself for believers in secularism.

NOTES

1. Sir Muhammded Iqbal, *The Reconstruction of Religious Thought in Islam* (London, 1934), p. 146.

2. E. I. J. Rosenthal, *Political Thought in Medieval Islam* (London: Cambridge University Press, 1962), p. 25.

3. Gustave E. von Grunebaum, *Islam and Medieval Hellenism* (London: Variorum Reprints, 1976), p. 445.

4. Vern L. Bullough, *Development of Medicine as a Profession* (New York: Karger Books & Science History Books, 1966), pp. 42-45. Charles Homer Haskins, *The Twelfth Century Renaissance* (Cambridge: Harvard University Press, 1927).

5. A. R. Gibb, *Mohammedism,* 2d ed. (New York: Galaxy Books, 1962), pp. 164-65.

6. Ignaz Goldziher, *Introduction to Islamic Theology*

and Law (Princeton: Princeton University Press, 1981), p. 77.

7. For a discussion of this see Malcolm H. Kerr, *Islamic Reform: The Political and Legal Theories of Mohammad Abduh and Rashid Rida* (Berkeley: University of California Press, 1966). Only one of Abduh's works has been translated into a Western language, in his case, French.

8. John L. Esposito, *Voices of a Resurgent Islam* (New York: Oxford University Press, 1983).

9. Several Qutb books are available in English. Much of this discussion is based on Yvonne Y. Haddad, "Sayyid Qutb: Ideologue of Islamic Revival," in Esposito, *Voices of a Resurgent Islam,* pp. 67-98.

10. Based on Charles J. Adams, "Mawdidi and the Islamic State," Esposito, pp. 99-133.

11. Iqbal, *op. cit.,* and John L. Esposito, "Muhammad Iqbal and the Islamic State," in Esposito, *Voices of a Resurgent Islam,* pp. 175-190.

12. Abdulaziz Sachedina, "Ali Shariati: Ideologue of the Iranian Revolution," in Esposito, *Voices of a Resurgent Islam,* pp. 191-214.

13. Quoted from "Survival of Islam in the Soviet Union," *A Background Brief* issued by the British Foreign and Commonwealth Office (London, March 7, 1987).

The Return of Mystical Dualism

Jean-Claude Pecker

Arthur Shopenhauer has quite clearly defined mysticism.[1] It is "a doctrine which aims at giving the direct feeling of what perception, concept, and in general any knowledge, are powerless to reach." Such a definition applies as well to religious mysticism, as to a more general mystical attitude, that is linked with the use of drugs, or with medium transes. In a sense, it covers also all kinds of parapsychological research.

One will not here comment much on the common features of the mystical attitude. They are well-known. In essence, mystical crisis is accompanied by organic or psychical disturbances, such as hysteric symptoms, or various hallucinations; there is no mysticism without ecstasy. Mysticism implies also a certain amount of repressed sexuality, as shown, for example, by the sayings of Saint-Jean de la Croix or Saint-Thérèse d'Avila. Mystical condition has displayed an alternating of exaltation and depression; in a sense, it shows indications of an illness of the will. Religious training, or education in a broader sense, is generally determining the intellectual representation associated with ecstasy or trance.

Although mysticism is often referred to as a way to knowledge, our own attitude is to deny it. We can justify this statement in a very clear way: As soon as one changes the intellectual framework of the mystical experience, one sees that the unity disappears; the Buddhist's ecstasy leads him to Nirvana. Saint-Thérèse's first visions were directly linked with Saint-Ignacius of Loyola's spiritual exercises; later on, they were modified through the strong influence of Saint-Jean de la Croix. The sufism of the Iranians is another form of mystical learning. Generally speaking, the mystics are plagiarizing each other, more or less consciously; hence, where do they find the "truth"? Their individual, natural, and innate tendencies are certainly a necessary ingredient in their mysticism; but nowhere do they find the "knowledge," and its expression, but in their education, readings, and training.

Strangely enough, one of the best known of the modern philosophers who have been speaking for mysticism's value, Henri Bergson,[2] admits it, possibly reluctantly: "We recognize that mystical experience, alone, cannot bring to the philosopher any final certainty." It would have a value only for he who "would be prepared to consider as likely the existence of a privileged experience, through which man could communicate with some transcendental principle." In other terms, one could be convinced only if one is already believing!

All of this is more or less admitted by the skeptics, and rationalists. As a matter of fact, as early as during the century of lights, philosophers admitted that the universe of knowledge was entirely within the realm of man's rational study of nature, and that religion, or mystical transes, could be only a way to the understanding of one's own psyche. That priests were reluctant to admit it has been true also, since that time; the two types of thinking were proceeding independently, but the scientist's universe was in essence self-sufficient.

For many historical reasons, on which we shall come back, it seems that modern-day science has more or less reversed this attitude. In some fields of science, one admits that there are parts of truth that are not to be known through science, but imply faith in some transcendental power, God, metascience or parascience, and the recourse to intuition, not to logic.

One field in which this attitude is clear-cut is astronomy. In essence, looking into the problems of the "origins" of the universe has led many to imply some idea about creation. Science of the universe, since the very early days of humankind, has been running a very long path. And we can briefly try to abstract it.

In the "beginning," the magic attitude was the most common; nothing was known about distance and size of heavenly bodies. One thing was known: in the form of storms, lightning, meteor showers, floods or fires, earthquakes, and thunder, the physical world was terrifying. It was natural enough to force us to respect it, to admit its power, to invent gods as representative of its strength. And of course, to worship and implore them. It became clear rather quickly that prayers were generally inefficient, and that gods were relatively insensitive to human miseries. In the meantime, humans observed the sky in an improved way; and they discovered both regularity and inflexibility: gods had to take a different image, above humans, and humankind had to accept its own complete dependence, in an absolute passivity. The submission to the absolute power of the sky was without any recourse; and this was the birth of astrology, the heavens being the strict masters of human destiny. It was also the reign of religions of eternity; the periodicities so far discovered gave the unavoidable and compelling idea that the universe, as a whole, was submitted to an infinite series of periodic returns. The Upanishads are definitely a periodic chronology that cover billions and billions of years. The Chinese yang-yin description is that of a perpetual alternation, a perpetual balance. The idea of eternity is far more tranquilizing than that of a universe limited in extent and duration.

The conquest of modern science has put aside the idea of the astrological influence, as the extension of the sky and the knowledge of the distances of stars made very unlikely this anthropocentric attitude on the part of the heavens. But it did not suppress the feeling for infinitude and eternity; quite the contrary. Some religious minds were, at first, shocked by this, even afraid. But they would not try to contradict it: "le silence éternel de ces espaces infinis m'effraie." Pascal was a sick man; but he was clearly expressing a very common feeling.

Still, in the beginning of this century, Albert Einstein was philosophically inclined to believe to an infinite and eternal universe. But it was clearly an extrapolation of the observed phenomena. However, Einstein had also written the equations for General Relativity, encompassing in a coherent doctrine the progress made within the framework of both universal gravitation and Special Relativity. Equations have many possible sets of solutions. Einstein wanted a static universe, one more likely to be eternal. Hence the solutions were well defined; an integration constant, named the cosmological constant, was necessary to insure that static nature. All was well in the best of all possible worlds, and we can take it literally!

But, at the same time, some new discoveries entered the picture. In the United States, Slipher discovered that the spectrum of distant galaxies was displaced toward the long wavelengths ("redshift"). Hubble found a way to determine their distance, and he found that the redshift was indeed proportional to distance. One physical phenomenon was able to explain such a shift: the so-called Doppler-Fizeau effect links any motion of the light source with a displacement of spectral lines. The displacement is proportional to the velocity of the source: it is a redshift in the case of receding velocities, and a blueshift in the case of approaching sources. Hence, Hubble could describe astronomical observations by referring to the "apparent velocities of receding galaxies." One had no other explanation than the Doppler effect; hence the adjective "apparent" quickly disappeared from the literature.

An obvious idea was to describe this universe of receding galaxies as a universe "in expansion," and to date the origin of this expansion, assuming it had been acting at a constant rate since it began. With the present values of the distance determinations, the "Hubble time," resulting from this backward extrapolation, is equal to something between 10 and 20 billions years.

In the same time, theoreticians, examining the Einstein's equations, have shown first that his static universe is unstable against changes in density, and, second, that the more general solutions to the equations were model universes in expansion after a unique explosion, assigned to the "primitive atom" by Cannon Lemaître. The word "Big-Bang" was later coined by Gamow and coworkers to describe this explosion. As the density was necessarily very high, it could be inferred that the temperature should also be very high, forbidding the existence of matter as it now appears. The physics of this very hot and very dense medium, in expansion, has been accurately described to predict some observable features, such as the chemical composition of present galaxies or the existence of background radiation throughout the sky. Both observations have indeed been made, and they have quantitatively shown that the Big Bang was adequate to describe many observed features of our universe. In the early fifties and sixties, the Big Bang acquired an aura of perfect honorability, and was accepted by almost every astronomer on Earth.[4] Quite naturally, it was immediately transformed into the best argument in favor of an initial creation, thus putting the Creation, as described at least symbolically in the Bible, into the realm of astronomy.

It is obvious that part of the universe was to be well-known through scientific investigations, but that another part was escaping this method, and was accessible only through some mystical experience or metaphysical intuition. But the two parts were linked at the time of the creation, science being, so-to-say, a clear-cut justification of religion, the "behind," or the "before" being more or less fitting the here and the now, in a satisfactory scientific match.

Illustrative of this attitude is this plea by Sir Edmund Whittaker:

These various computations are converging towards the conclusion that an epoch was, one or ten billions years ago, before which the Cosmos, if in existence, was under a form completely different from all that is known to us: thus this epoch represents the ultimate limit of science. We possibly may, without impropriety, refer to it as the creation. . . . It might very well be that this will be considered as the most important discovery of our times, since it represents a fundamental change in the scientific conception of the universe, similar to the one which has resulted, four centuries ago, from the work of Copernicus.[5]

The last sentence is, in my opinion, somewhat ironic!

And a follower of Sir Edmund, strangely but significantly enough, has been his holiness Pius XII:

It seems indeed that modern science, going backward one million centuries, has succeeded in being the witness for this "Fiat Lux" of the origins, for this instant at which an ocean of light rises from nothing, with matter . . . . Thus, Creation at a time; and for this, a Creator; hence, God! There thus comes, as implicit and imperfect as it may be, the word that we asked from science, and that the present human generation is expecting from it.[6]

I shall certainly not argue with the Big Bang cosmology at this point. Let us only say that most of the astronomers, though not all, have adopted this view, or similar derived views, of the universe's fate. Some of them have creation in mind, others do not (they consider the Big Bang only a moment in the past); still others consider that near the Big Bang, time is not well defined and that all ideas about the Big Bang being a single event in time and space are without any real meaning.

Among those who did not like the standard view of the Big Bang—for metaphysical reasons like Einstein—let us quote the typical ideas of Hoyle and his coworkers. Instead of some initial creation, they have decided that they want both an expanding universe and a static universe; hence, all matter destroyed had to be replaced by some new matter, on the spot. One had to appeal to the concept of "continuous creation."

Needless to say, the Big Bang has some creationist connotations, but they are by no means necessary. One can, in this respect, quote a typical theologian among the scholastic school, i.e., Saint Thomas Aquinas. The basic idea of the scholastic was to find or force an agreement between faith and reason, but the difficulties were significant. Aquinas opposed his contemporary Saint Bonaventure in a very clear way. In essence, he warned against confusing two quite different problems: the question of origins, and that of creation. Later on, the dilemma was brushed away for a time. In the fourteenth century, it appeared to the Ockhamists that one could indeed reconcile Aristotelianism with the dogmas of Christianity, but this led directly to the end of Ockhamism and the beginning of modern thought. The fact that Saint Thomas' warning in the preface of Pius XII's statement is still valid indicates more or less that we are back to the old quarrel between the scholastics—i.e., Saint Thomas on one side, Saint Bonaventure on the other side. Back to the Dark Ages.

What is clear through both the analysis of modern cosmology and that of modern physics is the microscopic universe. Uncertain relations are a way to escape classical determinism; they imply the existence of free will (on the part of particle's). The free will of particles, or the free will of divinity?

In biology the free will of man is in itself a strong argument for the transcendental being compatible with biological processes. I shall not comment on these, being neither a physicist nor a biologist. I would like only to note that new developments, such as the theory of strange attractors and the determinitic way to build chaos from an initial orderly situation when a great number of parameters are entering the problem (N-particle problems), might give a completely new turn to these sciences, a turn toward rationality. But it may be too early to discuss it.

Having thus bowed to the idea of creation, some modern cosmologists ask the very question raised more than 2,000 years ago by Plato: If the world has been created, "in the likeness of what animal did the creator make the world"? In the likeness or at least, at the intention of? Plato's reply, in a sense, was more acceptable than that of the neo-creationists. Plato's reply is clear: "The deity intending to make this world like the fairest and most perfect of intelligible beings, framed one visible animal comprehending within itself all other animals of a kindred nature." The unity of the universe is thus the reply to the urge for it to be an "intelligible" one. There is no mention of humans in this view; the world itself has to be this intelligible perfect animal; but Plato at least wanted some intention from the creator. The look for final causes is now enjoying a strong revival under the form of the so-called anthropic principle, in both its strong and weak forms.

The anthropic principle—a word coined some twenty years ago by Carter[9]—can be expressed in various ways, some more naive, but possibly more accurate than others. It is a reply to the often formulated question: "Why is the universe as it is?"—a typically metaphysical question as opposed to the "whence" and the "how." Carter's reply, an elaboration of a proposal of Dicke[10], is in some sense a return back to the times where man was considered the center and the purpose of the Christian universe; it erases four centuries of "objectivism." Carter says: "The presence of observers in the universe impose constraints, not only upon the age of the universe, from which the observers can appear, but also upon the set of its characteristics and fundamental parameters of the physics which takes place within it." Collins and Hawking[11] are implicitly going one step further: "Since it would be that the existence of galacies is a necessary condition for the development of intelligent life, the answer to the question "Why is the universe isotropic?" is "Because we are here!"

The need for this new way of thinking is manyfold. On one side, the difficulties of the standard cosmology, the isotropy of the background radiation, for example, had asked, for nonstandard models, the so-called inflationary universe (see Demaret and Barbier[12]). Collins and Hawking try to express this need by stating in essence that the initial conditions implied by a model of the universe compatible with the apparent present-day isotropy are very well defined, very limited; any departure from them would as a consequence forbid the formation of galaxies, stars, and planets, hence the apparition of life.

The second important argument (introduced in science by Dirac,[13] after Eddington) rests upon the constellation of coincidences of a numerical nature between various combinations of physical constants. In short, let us define three "big numbers" N_1, N_2, N_3, as follows:

$$N_1 = (hc/G\, m_p{}^2) \quad N_2 = 2_p\, (c/H_0)/(h/m_pc) \quad N_3 = (M_U/m_p)$$

Inverse of the constant of the fine structure of the electromagnetic interaction	size of the actual and observable universe	size of the proton, or the length of the Compton wave	the mass of the universe, in terms of the mass of the proton

One has $N_3 = N_1 = N_2 = 10^{80}$

One should note that these coincidences are not perfect, by far; the concept of "order of magnitude" is somewhat flexible. Moreover, as noted by De Vaucouleurs,[14] from a set of possible combinations of some given numbers, one can get any coincidence that is wanted, or almost. Nevertheless, the idea (a good one perhaps, or perhaps not!) was that links between macro- and microphysics were very strong; Dirac elaborated it by saying that all dimensionless numbers that can be constructed from the fundamental constants of physics are, at any time, connected by relations in which the coefficients are of the order unity; and these large numbers change with time. Even more, Dicke,[10] in contradistinction with Dirac, explicitly states that the coincidence $N_1 = N_2$ is a consequence of the presence of living creatures in the universe, and that it does not hold at any time, but only when conditions needed for life are present. This coincidence would characterize any universe containing observers, and able to be observed by them ("cognizable universe"). Later on, Rees and Carr have gone as far as to introduce the size of man, and other quantities linked with man, among the "other" fundamental constants of physics. The very fact that one can do such things, finding new coincidences, does seem to me very highly questionable;

after all, the forms of life are not well defined, but they cover a continuum from, say, the flea to the whale! Using this flexibility as a definition of the so-called order of magnitude, one can indeed prove anything, and its contrary!

This naturally led to the anthropic principle. Its weak form stipulates that the presence of observers in the universe impose constraints upon the temporal location of the latter. Its strong form is more speculative of course: Presence of observers in the universe imposes constraints not only upon their temporal location but upon the complete set of the properties of the universe.

There is no way to discuss these kinds of principle in a sensible way. Either one considers them as truisms (we are here, and this defines, no doubt, the conditions of the present day universe—at least it defines a set of possible conditions; a deterministic view that more or less defines its initial conditions) or as metaphysical dreams (the universe is such in order to, with the intention of, with the purpose of, allowing for our presence). In other words, I do not feel there is anything to discuss; one is or one is not a believer, period. Science needs God or it does not. I do not think, however, that people have really pointed out how this anthropic principle is, in essence, in contradistinction with the Copenhagen school of thought; how much it brings us back to a clear-cut determinism. One should note in this connection, that other more physical arguments are also bringing us to a sort of determinism; the essential difference is that on one side, the deterministic idea brings us back to a single universe, origin, or creation. On the other side, one should not rule out the possibility of a nondeterministic universe, an eternal one, such as described nowadays by some unorthodox cosmologies. At least, the anthropic principle rules out, as Einstein did, but for completely opposite reasons, a God who would indeed place dice.

The strong anthropic principle has some predictable and observable physical consequences. One of them is the prediction of the observed ratio between the number of photons and the number of protons in the present-day universe. Another one is the prediction of the possible range for the values of the mass of elementary particles. True these data are only *a posteriori* justifications of a certain number of properties of our universe. Hence they do not really have the status of scientific argument. In order to get rid of the anthropomorphic creation, the idea of "sets of subuniverses" has been introduced. In each separate subuniverse the initial conditions are different; they cover all possible combinations of parameters but only a very few of them are able to evolve into a "cognizable" universe, such as ours. But if these universes are without any mutual interaction, there is no point in considering them; and if they do not interact, then the principles of thermodynamics would have to be reformulated entirely. The physical arrow of time would be going in opposite directions in the two subuniverses.

In any case, in the absence of evidence for such neighboring universes, the reasoning can go no further except by saying that if we see the idealistic background of the anthropic principle, we still see nothing more in it than a truism, one linked with the description of the universe as a single cosmic event, a description that has been shown to lead to a sort of mystical duality quite naturally present in the anthropic principle itself.

Whatever the various aspects of it, the dualism is present in many aspects of modern science. It needs, in cosmology, the determinism linking God's will and human presence; in microphysics, it needs, on the contrary, the concept of a gambling God. In all cases, it introduces God behind a physical process, linking the world of physical observation and that of transcendental intuition. As a matter of fact, God *is* this link, intrinsically needed in order to reconcile completely religion and science. Clearly, this is for us a case of an *ad hoc* recuperation, which has no value.

Having more or less diagnosed the illness, we must now ask the question: Why? Indeed, it is not easy to reply. At the end of the last century, confidence in the power of science was tremendously strong, and religion was losing its claim to be linked with the physical world. Of course, the secular religions were also fearing the loss of convincing influence; evolutionism or transformism, after the dating of geological strata, the complexity of microphysics, the very enormity of the universe, and the universe considered as eternal and infinite—these were indeed devastating.

When our operational knowledge of physics and astronomy was rising so fast in the first part of this century, doubts as to determinism (the Copenhagen school), doubts as to infinity (Einstein himself), as regarding eternity (the expanding universe) have opened a door to the return of religion within the realm of science. It went so far as to allow the teaching of neo-creationism in some American states, on the same footing as evolution.

I wonder whether this new rise of mysticism has not taken its roots in a typical feature of the modern world: fear of science. Since the beginning of the century, novels have constantly shown science under its black cloud. The scientists are ridiculous or they are monsters: Frankenstein was, in the last century, a precursor indeed, and since that time, we have had many Frankensteins and Folamours. The fantastic and terrible visitors from outer space, described by H. G. Wells, were also a sign of this fear. Behind the obvious confidence in scientific progress, as displayed by the works of Jules Verne, is hidden another aspect of his novels: scientists are dangerous and crazy—from Camaret to Lindenbrock, from J. T. Mason to Rodolphe de Gortz, from Dr. Ox to Zephryn Xyrdal.

The dangerous scientist is nowadays not even hidden by the beneficial effects of science. In the nineteenth century, it was the triumph of Pasteur, electricity in the countryside, fast and comfortable transportation. Now, science takes on a different connotation: it is the gas war, or, still worse, Hiroshima; it is pollution of all kinds, the failure to cure cancer, and the appearance of new illnesses, such as AIDS. We cannot erase science, and its predictive value, yet we continuously complain of this dry modern world of technique, to which a soul is missing. The tendency is to strive, against all evidence, for a reconciliation of scientific knowledge with a mental effort toward a better human world, between science and morals, between science and God, between Prometheus and Zeus.

In other words, I feel the trend is linked not so much with the progress of scientific knowledge, but more closely with the historical situation.

It is interesting to note that the mystical dualism we see blooming complements a renewed belief in the reality of the supernatural, although this was not a logical necessity. By letting the physical reality be complemented by a mystical reality has opened the door to the belief that mystical reality could sometimes overcome the usual view of rational reality and be shown through miracles, or through the paranormal. Some well-known theologians, such as F. Russo, went so far as to justify[16] the alleged existence of telekinesis (the spoon bending "experiment)" via miracles, apparently in opposition to the laws of physics, but belonging to the world of the supernatural. He concludes:

We measure well, and we ask that others measure well, what is implied by the recognition of the reality of PSI phenomena. That is, the existence, besides the category of phenomena which one thought so far they constituted the whole of positive reality, of another category of phenomena distinctly different from "natural" phenomena. Certainly religious and philosophical thought claim the existence, outside of the positive realities, which are the only ones science knows, of some other entities. But the latter are not located in the realm of phenomena, although it is conceivable they might interfere with them. Now, with PSI phenomena, we are in front of positive entities, at least in their manifestations. It is not surprising therefore that science does not accept easily to let them a place. But facts are there. We must submit to them.

It is of course impossible for us[17] to follow these extreme views. As a matter of fact, the concept of physical reality is one that can be discussed thoroughly without mystical connotation. The modern neo-positivists (Carnap and the Vienna circle, or Popper, in spite of many differences) refuse to oppose (and synthesize) the natural sciences and sciences of the mind—to oppose and then to reconcile—they defend a rational concept of reality.[18]

Mystical dualism thus appears often as mystification. And, taking into account the fact that the strange ways of para-science are the natural (if not completely logical) consequence of the modern return to mystical dualism, it is impossible not to be shocked at this resurgence, and not to warn today's layman against the coming dark ages.

NOTES

1. See the articles "Mysticisme" and "Mystique expéri-ence" in: *Dictionnaire Rationaliste,* Nouvelles Editions Rationalistes, 1981, Paris, nouvelle édition.
2. Bergson, Henri, 1935, *Les Deux Sources de la Morale*

et de la Religion (The Two Sources of Morality and Religion), Greenwood Press.

3. A very extended bibliography is given in: Jaki, Stanley L., 1974, *Science and Creation,* Scott. Acad. Press.

4. For a descripton of the Big Bang, other classical cosmologies, and unorthodox cosmologies, read J. Schneider, 1986, *Cosmologie,* in *La Nouvelle Encyclopédie,* Fayard, Paris, or J.-C. Pecker, 1985, *Encyclopedia Univeralis, Symposium,* La Nature de l'Univers, p. 279–293.

5. Whittaker, E., 1946, *Space and Spirit,* p. 118–119.

6. Pius XII, 1951, 22 nov, Discours à l'Académie Pontificale des Sciences. (My translation; the original is in French.)

7. Saint Thomas of Aquinas, (1225–1274), *Summa Theologica I,* question 46 a.2.; and *"De aeternitate Mundi contra murmurentes."*

8. Plato, *Timaeus.*

9. Carter, B., 1974, *IAU Symposiuum* n[63], Longiar ed., Reidel Publ., p. 291, (the same idea is expressed in an unpublished paper, dated 1967).

10. Dicke, R. M., 1961, *Nature, 192,* 440.

11. Collins, C. B., Hawking, S. W., 1973, *Astrophys. J., 180,* 317.

12. Demaret, J., Barbier, C., 1981, *Rev. Quest. Scient. 152,* 181–22.

13. Dirac, P. A. M., 1937, *Nature, 139,* 23; Dirac, P. A. M., 1974, *Proc. Ro. Soc. A. 338,* 439.

14. De Vaucouleurs, G., nov-déc, 1948, *l'Astronomie.* p. 224.

15. Rees, M. J., Carr, B. J., 1979, *Nature, 278,* 605–612.

16. Russo, F., *Etudes,* 1978, July, Paris.

17. One can find a bibliographical review on the paranormal in: Pecker, J.-C., 1982, *Le débat sur les phénomènes paranourmax, Proble* Politiques et Sociux, n[0]

450, Docum. Française, Paris.

18. A good bibliography is contained in: Bayonas, A., pp. 1–44, in *The Concept of Physical Reality,* Ed. Bitaskis, E., Zacharopoulos, Publi., Athens, 1983.

The Dilemma of Fundamentalism

Alberto Hidalgo Tuñon

The so-called "higher religions" are facing a challenge not easily surmountable. The success of the scientific outlook finds them compelled to launch an unchanging ideological attack against the unforgiving, critical, and materialistic thought, which underlies such a view. Thus they ought to try to encourage their faith by means of a backward step in their sources, through strengthening their traditions, and by saving the value system that in earlier times granted them a renewed energy and great social influence.

Nevertheless, this backward step in the sources can lead fundamentalists to unqualified and irrational acceptance of the rites and myths of which they are an outcome. By doing this, they are led away from the conciliatory process with scientific and philosophical reason, whose realistic assimilation allowed them thus far to adapt to the modern world and to survive in it. Strictly speaking, therefore, the "higher religions" would become the "lowest religions," because they would bring back to life such primitive patterns of religiosity as fetishism, animism, the zoomorphic cultism, and so on.

The fundamentalist movement's dilemma, consequently, which underlines its contemporary orthodoxy and its reactionary stage, can be explained in this way: If the higher religions go on assuming the scientific outlook and its

71

epistemological background, they risk crashing against
nontheism's Scylla, which would ruin the essential core of
their faith; but, if they do not become scientific, and go on
struggling openly against free inquiry, then they venture upon
a reactionary enterprise, which will lead them to be wrecked
by the Charybdis of mythology and irrationality. Now they
must choose. Many fundamentalists seem to be reactionary.
However, like so many large-scale social movements,
fundamentalism is not a unified religious position; the
clustering of faiths and intellectual frameworks that support
them seem to reach an agreement at this point. I shall try
to explain in socio-cultural terms the reasons underlying the
contemporary dilemma of higher religions. I shall argue that
to understand the dilemma, it is convenient to conceptualize
the anthropological development of the religious phenomenon
from an evolutionary perspective.

The remaining pages are devoted to exploring the
functional and disfunctional consequences that could be
derived from fundamentalist irrationalism. The discovery of
latent functions will provide other means of explaining the
ways in which the "unintended consequences" of fundamentalist action could perform positive functions within the
context of the world social system.

THE EVOLUTIONARY STAGES OF RELIGIONS

Between the various historical typologies that the anthropological sciences and the philosophies of religions have created
to explain the development of this extraordinary cultural
phenomenon, I will single out, because of its elegance and
its depth, the one proposed by Dr. Gustavo Bueno.[1] At this
point, it is enough to provide a concise introduction.

Many authors—including radical humanists—agree that religion produces tremendous and powerful emotions and unleashes affective forces and mental transformations in practically all human beings. Thus, the religious experience is generally regarded as a cultural universal. Along this line, Edward O. Wilson has acknowledged that a primary source of biological power exists in religion.[2] It is possible, therefore, to understand the origins of social and religious patterns in Darwinian terms. But, while Dr. Wilson is right to emphasize that "sacred rituals are the most distinctively human" and that, in spite of this, they are "materialistic phenomena" intelligible via evolution, his reductivist stance seems exaggerated.

I agree with Wilson that recognizing an originary force in religions, whose empirical manifestations are observable, does not imply that they become a mysterious phenomenon. Mythological religious explanations are not worth mentioning from the scientific and philosophical view, both of which face this enigma of free inquiry. But the materialistic approach does not require assuming that there are *specific human culturgenes* for explaining the universality of the religious features in sociocultural systems. The common observation that religious beliefs, like so many other ideological convictions, can affect behavior, does not require other biological procedures different from those *generic physical brain mechanisms,* which any social learning requires. If it is not so, then a man who changes his mind or converts to religion should be suffering a genetical switch, which would not be compatible with "the epigenetic rules."

However, I do not insist here that Wilson's perspective regarding the explanation of the behavioral and social basis of religion—advanced in the past and illustrated by materialistic thinkers such as Hume, Marx, Feuerbach, or Freud—rest upon acknowledging a primary source of religiosity. As he so eloquently puts it:

But religion itself will endure for a long time as a vital
force in society. Like the mythical giant Anteus who drew
energy from his mother, the earth, religion cannot be
defeated by those who merely cast it down. The spiritual
weakness of scientific materialism is due to the fact it has
no such primal source of power.[3]

In this sense, the key question is: What is the nature
of this source of originary power? In my opinion, we must
seek a religious originary experience in the primitive man's
living conditions. The handicap of the traditional illustrated
approach is based on their unadmission that there is a genuine
religious experience, but they mistakenly imagine that all
experiences of this kind are based upon delusions, alienation,
fallacy, or fraud. The critical theorists of religions argue in
their writings that these are elements of the economical, social
and/or psychological superstructure. These were seen as the
sources of human alienation: a cognitive wedge is driven
between man's consciousness and the objectified social world,
so that man sees what are essentially creations of his own
consciousness in the form of hard, dominating, external
realities. The religious beliefs stand as seemingly independent
and alienating forces, created by man, yet reflecting back upon
him as independent presences. Thus it is a question of
"mystified" experience. Wilson, though firmly located in this
materialistic intellectual tradition, refuses its oversimplification
and asks himself about more ontological depth and powerful
foundations of religions. For him, "religion is a great deal
more than just the opium of the people, the happy pill for
people to take during rites of passage—death, marriage, and
so on."[4] If it were only that, it would have an end in the
USSR for instance. As a matter of fact, he argues that the
emotional power of religion is too easily captured by
nationalism and the fantasies of madmen. If we talk about
recent processes of change, as in Iran, where Muslim religion

has become the substance in a new sea of fanaticism capable of leading its followers to suicidal action, then we would be in the presence of a perfect counter-demonstration of economic determinism.

What, then, is the nature of the source of religious originary power? In recent years, Dr. Marvin Harris[5] has furnished an interpretation of the role of religions in sociocultural evolution explicitly aimed at disassociating his Cultural Materialism approach from Marx's most famous remark on the subject. As he pointed out:

> It is ironic, therefore, that Marx should have characterized religion as the "opium of the people." Under conditions appropriate for the development of messianic leadership, religion again and again has proved itself capable of organizing downtrodden and exploited masses into revolutionary armies.[6]

Harris emphasizes the phrase "under conditions appropriate," because this is what he means by *feedback* between infrastructure and superstructure. Thus religion can be system-maintaining or system-destroying depending on the balance of optimizations and conflicting interest in the rest of the system, that is, in conformity with the limitations imposed on it by the infrastructure. Consequently, the ideas of Harris, *malgré lui,* are extremely similar to Karl Marx's dialectic, so that infrastructure is determinant in the first, as well as the last instance and because religion lacks any source of independent power outside of a sociocultural fixed system. From this viewpoint the Islamic revitalization is not to be found in the religious project of the Ayatollah Khomeini, but rather in the despotic and exploitative colonial infrastructure imposed on Iran in the aftermath of the Second World War. "Similarly," said Harris, "the future of Iran's Islamic Republic will not be settled by the fundamentalism of the Muslims, but by the secularizing trends of industrialization."[7]

Nor is it clear why the religious beliefs are so affective and effective in unleashing such powerful social forces in the masses, if religions lack any source of autonomous power. Why do sacred rituals, rather than economic, political, social, and others, entail typically the most complicated domain of culture in each society? It seems to need a backward step in human nature, as Wilson proposes, to seek the ontolgoical roots on which the vital force of religion is found. Though there is no doubt that as a general rule economic progress and "modernization" undergo a secularization process, still it remains to be explained why the exceptions to this rule are so frequent and why a large number of philosophers, scientists, and others who maintain a natural scientific approach to their problems, are able to be subjective and honest believers. Is it a case of simple alienation? In my opinion, Harris mistakes the theology, which is obviously concerned with the superstructure, and the true religious feeling, the nature of which he has not investigated sufficiently.

At this point, Gustavo Bueno's evolutionary theory of religion supplies an intermediate and materialistic response between Wilson's biological theory and the cultural thesis of Harris. I would label this response as an etological one, but not generic. However, I would be mistaken if I did not add that Bueno obtained this response for a *dialectical regressus* from the contemporary stage. Understanding religion is not independent of observation and explanation as to its various historic features. What religions are nowadays depends on the evolutionary display of their essential *nucleum* in a cultural *body* and a cultural *course*, which is mutually determined. This essential nucleum must be tracked back to the originary experiences of etological interspecific character. It is possible on this view to deal with the phenomenological approach of the so-called science of religions (inspired by Edmund Husserl, Max Scheler, Rudolf Otto, and other German thinkers) and the scientific outcome of Cultural Materialism and Prehistory, whenever the traditional link between God and religions, started by higher religions, are broken. What the phenomenologists have called *Das Heilege* (that which is holy) or the *numen* is not, therefore, a God or a human being.

Thus, what is the *nucleum* of religions? Bueno's idea is that the religious life of man began with intercourse between the primitive human groups and some kind of animals in the Paleolithic time. Usually a religious meaning is attributed to cafe paintings of Paleolithic time, and there are various explanations in this sense to interpret the cultural significance of such worthy vestiges: sympathetic magic, fetishism, and so on. In fact, these wild animals represented for Paleolithic man entities that, without humanity, are centers of will and mind; entities that they should deceive, plead with, obey, or kill according to circumstances. Gustavo Bueno proves this thesis with a great deal of ethnographic and bibliographical material in his book *The Divine Virago*.

It is interesting to emphasize here the dialectical way in which he turns upside down the classical *ex actibus religiosis* argument of phenomenology in favor of the religious truth. As is well known, phenomenology is based upon a fundamental questioning of the spontaneous and naturalistic attitudes that characterize everyday life and the realms of natural science. The task of epistemology, in his position, is to explore and reveal the essential types and structures of experience because subjective experience is the source of all objectivities. Phenomenology seeks to delve into experiences and to clarify the very ground of knowledge. In this endeavor the methods of "direct intuition" and "insight into essential structures" are offered as the principal means of penetrating the depths of consciousness and transcending the world of everyday affairs. As I have already noted, the phenomenological science of religion considers that specifically religious knowledge appears linked to some terrifying experiences, that is, the so-called "experiences of fear and trembling" in the presence of the *holy* or the *numinic*. If this is so, the main question that arises is: What kind of real entities can be reputed to have a capacity for stirring up such a terrifying emotion? Indeed, in the strictly scientific level it is only possible to testify to the real existence of wild animals whose presence prehistoric man held as a "direct intuition" and a "dreadful insight." If the phenomenological science of religion will assume the worthy scientific status, which it claims, it must accept this conclusion.

The *primary* or nuclear stage of religion concludes with the domestication of animals. The agricultural revolution in Neolithic times had generated a passage to the pattern of *secondary* religiosity, that is, to the religions of *Gods-dema,* those who went through "from the beginning of time" and to those primitive farming people who still worship in the tropics. Again this thesis seems to accord with the outcome of paleontology, ethnology, the history of religions, astronomy, and other sciences. The shapes of wild animals represented in the vault of caves project themselves in the vault of heaven (as zodiacal signs), but maintaining by inversion their numinic breeze and acquiring by expansion a delirious character. This light-headed, but not disfunctional, feature of mythic-poetical religion ought to be considered as based on mistaken and alienating beliefs. Therefore, they decompose slowly in the presence of rationalistic and scientific criticism. It is extremely significant that countries such as India hold a weak and insufficient penetration of scientific outlook and associated technological changes; the mythological religions will develop their inexorable arrangement among the poor, the uneducated, and the romantics. Unless a change of the ecological, technological, political, and economic conditions takes place, the religions will not suffer the whole passage of "reorganization," which will be distinctive of their *third* stage.

Therefore, the changes in human living conditions have been in connection with the appearance and the diffusion of the first scientific categories, those which have stopped the superstitious delirium and have caused the passage from the *zoomorphic* Gods to *anthropomorphic* ones. It is the passage from the *mythological* stage to the *theological* stage. Nevertheless, it is difficult to treat the abundance and complexity of historical, anthropological, and bibliographical change. In classical philosophy it is customary to talk of the passage *from myth to logos*.[8] This problem cannot be understood as canceled because of the development of Western civilization, as the present ideological rearmament of fundamentalism clearly reveals.

Let us be precise about this matter. It seems verified that the majority of the highest religions consolidated their beliefs around the sixth century B.C.E. The existentialist philosopher Karl Jaspers has conceptualized this switch with the "Time-Axis" notion.[9] The "Time-Axis" notion suggests that at about the sixth or fifth century B.C.E. various cultural facts arose simultaneously, which moved up the historical course of "humanity." These facts are fundamentally a new kind of religion, such as those represented by Lao-Tse and Confucius in China, by Buddha in India, by Zoroaster in Persia, by King Numa Pompilius in ancient Rome, by the great prophets of Israel, and others. What is the reason for this cultural change? Jasper seeks the cause in a metaphysical influence of a certain mysterious and "surrounding esprit" on "humanity." It seems very unlikely that Jaspers could prove this thesis, because his response is not a genuine, but a spurious explanation. On the contrary, scientific materialism can explain much better, by means of infrastructural causes, the process of mythological simplification, which led, on the one hand, to the construction of rational theologies (henotheists and/or monotheists), and on the other, to the emergence of the forceful Greek free inquiry whose leaders we bring to mind at the Humanist Pantheon.

It is of course true that theological activity has been involved in the beginning with scientific and philosophical activities. Nevertheless, it has not been a divino lash of the "surrounding," which has whipped a metaphysical "humanity" and has been the cause of its rational reaction, but technological mechanisms (for instance, the diffusion of the Iron Culture as John D. Bernal puts it[10]), scientific ones (as the development of astronomy, arithmetic, geometry, etc.), and, mainly, infrastructural factors, such as the demographic and economic ones. In this last sense, Marvin Harris emphasizes convincingly that "the end of animal sacrifice coincided with the development of the universal and spiritualized religions."[11] From a historical and cultural view, Harris argues that the main universalist religions share in common great expansive empires, the politics and the dietetic sanctions of which maintain the economical stability of their respective systems. Thus, this religious passage involves an evolutionary development and a former consolidation of the bureaucratic states and "hydraulic societies" (Wittfogel). It is not very odd, therefore, that there have been chronological and structural differences between the cultural evolution of the Asiatic empires, for instance, and Meso-American civilization, according to infrastructural circumstances. Hence, the fact that the "Time-Axis" notion turns out a confused and useless concept, because it is founded on a vague and abstract "humanity," as a whole, in which the contrasting strategies followed by several cultural circles involving the same problems during various times have been ignored.

In line with Harris, the universal religions of love and

compassion have been started in the Old World by means of a change of divine power from the animals, assumed as sources of food and proteins to the persons of "great suppliers," to those who slaughter and distribute them to the people, and increase their influence. When the ancient "great suppliers" come to be more and more unable to substantiate their majesty by means of popular shows of bountiful magnanimity, they encourage the people to seek spiritual rewards in the future life. As an instance of this spiritual passage Harris mentions Buddhism and Jainism.

Consequently, the *third stage* of religion is based on this complex process, which led from the agricultural Gods-dema to the spiritualized shapes of abstract divinities. Cultural Materialism's explanation is consistent on this point with the evolution of religions sketched here, inasmuch as it sets a cultural link between the extinction of animal sacrifice and the beginning of higher religions. However, this link is still too eternal and generic to explain the rational character of the cessation of superstitious deliriums. The ideological shrewdness and the powerful will of the "great suppliers" is not enough to produce this deep change. They could only encourage the people to seek spiritual rewards with one single condition: that the cultural circumstances facilitate it and that this "reorientation" should possess credibility.

What new circumstances have arisen for such a change to be accepted? At this point Bueno's evolutionary thesis alludes to two specific circumstances, which, without deserting materialism, enjoy a dialectical feature. These are: (1) the facing confluence of mythological worlds almost never compatible; and (2) the start of a naturalistic pattern of explanation. I will quote *in extenso* Bueno's typical way of thinking:

From this confluences could come out (. . .) the main criticial stimulus ("from myth to logos") for the theologians and, next, for the philosophers, shocked at that which someone could be considered the height of paradox, namely: that the *final monotheism* of the third stage of religion continues to be multiple, *polytheist* (Yahweh, Alah. . . .). The process of simplification (the limit of which is monotheism), as a medical treatment for the delirious, is linked to the political interplay between the States with purpose to become *Universal States,* and also will be reflected within each mythological sphere. The paradox mentioned multiplies itself extensively: it is the paradox of polytheism (ethical, ontological) *of the highest gods.*[12]

But Gustavo Bueno emphasizes a second circumstance:

Only when new *impersonal models* of meteorolgoical, astronomical and cosmological constructions have been brought to perfection, then can there be a perspective to insert a new *discipline* at the mythological delirium (which have organized the *cosmos* in outstanding accordance with parental *relationship).* . . . *The naturalistic models* (for instance, the Phoenician poem of Sanchunjaton) and, particularly, the *geometrical patterns,* which have performed the presocratic metaphysic should be those tools which could remove the *mythological delirium* from its closing.[13]

This has a relevant consequence for us. If it is right that the more rational and higher religions, in particular those which support a unique and intangible God (such as in Buddhism, Christianity, and Islam), have taken place from the naturalistic pattern of rationality, then they carry within themselves the germ of atheism. This philosophical germ has occurred afterwards, taking form since the natural theology of Aristotle toward the so-called "theology of God's death," today developed in Christianity.

I think that from the evolutionary approach of religions sketched here the dilemma of fundamentalism can be understood. The higher religions are on the *threshold of atheism;* their leaders draw tighter with scientific humanism and assume its epistemological background; eventually this will mean the ruin of their attempt, because the limiting idea of an intangible God and the mystery, which is still perpetuated in their stylized rituals, could vanish in the horizon of the atheism. Thus, it is not too odd that, from our evolutionary and materialistic perspective, they opted for the fundamentalist strategy. As will be made clear from the discussion above, this strategy implies the backward step in their sources, that is, in the *secondary* or *primary* stages of religion. It also implies the open struggle against the scientific and philosophical outlook, which had led them to the present third stage. But then, what consequences are derived from this reactionary strategy? Are the fundamentalists conscious of the irrational and mythical course they have adopted?

FUNCTIONS AND DISFUNCTIONS OF FUNDAMENTALISM

In the previous section, I described the evolutionary nature of religion, tracing its broad line of development from its nuclear state to the present. I will locate the contemporary revival of religious fundamentalism within this context. Since religion has a real evolutionary basis, I am afraid that the scientific outlook cannot ruin it, but only disturb and convert its originary experience into other forms of collective experience. An indication of this transformation is, as Bueno's book points out, the new feeling toward animals, which has become apparent in the formation of animal liberation fronts and in the proliferation of animal protection societies as well as ecological movements.[14] In the recent years animal abuse has been viewed as beneath contempt, and many penal codes consider cruelty toward animals to be a crime. It is the tremendous development of the new science of ethology and the success of the scientific outlook on religiosity, so that it is impossible to say, copying Feuerbach's sharp formulation, that nowadays "the mystery of the Theology is the Ethology."

Another indication of this transformation is the religious meaning that is usually attributed to the experience, appearance, and *revelation* of the unearthly or supernatural visitors. The extraordinary rise of interest in unidentified flying objects in industrial and technological societies can be interpreted as a certain flow back toward mythologizing the world. The recent and plentiful literature concerning *UFOlogy* is impregnated with a certain religious feeling about miracles, secrecy, liturgical rites, goodwill messages, divine reminders, policy, and the like. Thus many prophets, deluded persons, and illuminati desire to go out to face the unknown, announce the "third awakening," or cry the arrival of guardian angels and hellenistic devils, the religious and mythical condition of which could hardly be disguised by their technological environment and by their cinematographic representation. Many traditional religions only require light mythological making-up to embody in their essential scope the beliefs in the interplanetary visitors as divine messengers, angels, or envoys of powerful cosmic deities, which are watching and providentially shielding humanity from space. On this subject Gustavo Bueno points out:

> The *UFOlogy* and the *Ethology* seems to us as two consequences—one in the plane of science fiction and the other in the plane of the strict science—of the same process, namely: *the backward step toward the pattern of primary and secondary religiosity,* when the *third stage* of religions,

mainly in the *form of exasperating Christian anthropocentrism,* seems to have exhausted their creative possibilities."[15]

That's not much progress toward understanding the contemporary fundamentalist movement; nevertheless, these indications of contemporary changes in the meaning of religiosity can lay down a pattern for measuring their evolutionary direction. Because, if the newest manifestations of religiosity, even when assuming the advances of scientific learning (Ethology, UFOlogy), could bring back to life the primitive standard of the primary and secondary stages of its evolution, then could fundamentalism do any differently? I don't think so. Unless something unexpected comes up, fundamentalism can only try to encourage the faithful by means of a backward step. Indeed, the strategy is not to embody the scientific outcomes, but to strengthen traditional beliefs against unforgiving and critical thought. Therefore, in its originary form, fundamentalism points toward the past rather than the future, and faces free inquiry and the new idea of science as a social and ideological danger for all religions and their spiritual power over human consciousness.

In contrast to other contemporary manifestations of religiosity, fundamentalism enjoys a great social influence, because it makes good use of the traditional and well-rooted organizations in various countries, and because it receives income and support of old intellectual frameworks and powerful conservative forces. Furthermore, the fundamentalist movement has a number of advantages compared to the scientifical outlook: the credulity and superstition of the people; the psychological safety, which provides their uncomplicated doctrines; and the sociological forces of passivity and uniformity, which avoid the rise of the deviate members. As long as the scientific culture does not penetrate

the habits of thinking and behavior of the religious, leaving
it to an elite few members of the Western upper-middle-class,
it is hardly to be expected that a fundamental change of
direction or a new stage of religion will arise. I cannot help
thinking, with Max Weber, that the progress of rationality
brought disenchantment to the world, but also that modernization caused the process of secularization.

According to this evolutionary view, what are the functions and disfunctions of fundamentalism? It is convenient
to distinguish two different models of fundamentalism: one
that characterizes religions within the well-developed countries,
where science and technology find themselves consolidated,
and the other that characterizes the religions that extend
through underdeveloped countries, where fundamentalism
without scientific rationality has become the substance in a
new sea of fanaticism. Both are resisting change and
modernization, but in doing so, they follow different roads.
Since religion, as a cultural phenomenon, neither grows nor
modifies the other elements of the total culture, it becomes
diachronic—an inexhaustible quarry of fossilized survival—
and *synchronic*—reliving ancestral experiences—which
acquire different features and functions, according to social,
economic, political, and epistemological circumstances.

Let us limit our scope to contemporary Western
fundamentalism, which defends religions becoming great
powers as forces of psychological adaptation and social
integration,[16] against the scientific and valueless materialism.
In particular, religious beliefs are shown within the free
countries as the touchstone of human rights and as the reliable
ground of political democracy. For instance, Carl E. Henry
apologizes for fundamentalism on political grounds in this way:

Religious liberty involves much more than the right to hold
one's faith and to express it both in worship and practice,

to propagate the Gospel and to persuade and teach others, and to give religious education to one's children. It embraces also the right to peaceful assembly and association, freedom of opinion and expression, freedom from arbitrary arrest and detention, and freedom to leave one's country and return. . . . *Thus the whole bastion of universal right and duties rest upon a theological basis.*"[17]

This fallacious reasoning can be considered as a sign of the Western fundamentalism's tactics in a double sense. First, if the traditional Judeo-Christian faith has provided the *only* adequate intellectual support for the life system of modern democratic societies, then a perpetual backward step toward their reliable biblical foundations (stated *in the past* during the period from 1100 B.C.E. to 150 C.E.) is *only* required for system-maintaining of these societies. Second, because the theological basis assumed for human rights *lacks scientific meaning* in all respects and mistakes an ideological speech for an explanation.

From a historical view, Paul Kurtz has completely refuted the idea that belief in democracy and freedom can be justified on biblical grounds. As a matter of fact, he argues that "the Bible can be and has been used to support virtually all political and social ideologies. It is surely difficult to find explicit textual bases for democratic freedom."[18] The Spaniards and, in general, the Europeans are well aware of the doctrine of "the divine right of Kings," and we know that the Catholic Church, while it was the more politically dominating institution, favored a repressive and punitive approach toward freedom of opinion and expression by means of the Inquisition, the *Index librorum prohibitorium,* censorship, and so on. Any fair report of the issue shows that the democratic system was a discovery of the ancient Greeks and that, in the recent history of the Western World, civil and political liberties were never conquered so long as philosophical and scientific rationality could emerge victorious over the various contradictory and heart-shaped religious beliefs. As Paul Kurtz put it:

> Pluralistic democracy developed in part as a response to the emergence of competing denominations and sects and also because of the development of secular, scientific, and naturalistic influences.[19]

The nonacceptance of credos and immutable dogmas has always been the critical temperament of free inquiry. In this sense Henry is right when he says that the "nontheistic view renders such (human) rights merely postulatory and problematic." But he is wrong when he assumes that this critical and nondogmatic support for human rights is intellectually weaker and in practice a less resolute and less engaged defense against their infringement than his opportunistic theological foundation *a posteriori*. If human rights and democratic liberties depend on either theologically or metaphysically transcendent sources, then their grounds are *heteronomous* ones (Kant). Thus, even though we declare these divine grounds as absolute, they will only have a *hypothetical* meaning, the value *subjectively* granted on these theological beliefs. Furthermore, when such sources rest on certain biblical history, it is a serious logical mistake to regard its precarious and contingent grounds as universal and necessary.

As far as we know the will of God is inscrutable and immeasurable, by definition, according to Judeo-Christian monotheism, and there is no method for its setting that interprets the biblical scripture. However, since there are biblically based interpretations, which make faith compatible with virtually every form of political order, whether dictatorship, autocracy, monarchy, oligarchy, or democracy, there is nothing to guarantee that the present and defensive democratic interpretation will remain unchanged. What the wind of God blows in another direction, justifying the insensitive extermination of his enemies, cannot be prevented. Hence the presumed intellectual support for human rights by biblical theism is much more precarious and less trustworthy than any other, including the nontheist intellectual support.

What is the essential reason for Western fundamentalism's new favor toward the democratic systems? From our evolutionary view, I think that it is borne out of senile decay. Since religion cannot impose its beliefs and value systems by force on Western societies, it ought to opt for undertaking the democratical system as an extraordinary method for saving traditions and defending originary faith through the unyielding stronghold of the *personal conscience.* Such is the right direction followed by Protestantism and by the traditional Catholic Church, which after Vatican II only acknowledged religious liberty as a *negative and private right* of every person to possess immunity from religious coercion and to decide individually and responsibly in matters regarding religious reality and truth. But, in sociocultural terms, if our evolutionary stages of religion are right, and if the higher religions are, as we affirmed in the above section, on the threshold of atheism, then this *retirement* toward subjectivity and this *ontological reduction* of the level of religious reality and truth to the stage of private conscience can only be interpreted as the *senile age of religions.*

However, because the new biochemical techniques of reviving can be democratically used for all social organizations, the higher religions will still endure a long time through their individual cells. Let's therefore interpret the main force of Henry's argument in this way: religion can be considered as the only democratic system maintaining independence from any infrastructural changes or scientific and rationalistic progress, because such *human* changes and external progress can neither disturb nor invade *man's inner spiritual life.* All *external* instances are irrelevant for the inviolable sacredness of human conscience, when it receives the right guidance of God's divine inspiration or his transcendent norms. While human science and human society are fallible, Christian science and God's City are eternal and infallible. Therefore, fortified within the trenches of personal conscience and the sure truthfulness of his faith, the Christian fundamentalist of the West not only profits unscrupulously from rights and freedom, which in earlier times he refused to agnostics, atheists, and rationalists, but cynically, discredits as dogmatic and as intolerant, the critical and rationalistic frame of mind, which painfully conquered these same rights and liberties, and which nowadays shelters theists and nontheists alike.

I would like to think that religious organizations are irrevocably engaged in the defense of liberty and democracy. When this happens in countries where human rights are grossly violated, such organizations—including fundamentalist ones—assume a *positive function*. But one should not seek the foundations of democracy in the biblical Scripture, where it can never be found. On the contrary, religious fundamentalism is *exclusive* and tolerates democratic liberties only when it cannot abolish them. In particular, it maintains an opposing position to the scientific outlook. Thus to call on democracy as a mechanism of defense for faith clearly takes on air an *obscurantism*. For instance, in the name of democracy fundamentalism claims that the "theory" of special creations should be taught alongside evolutionary biology, faith-healing alongside medicine, and so on.[20] Furthermore, like pseudoscience, magic, or witchcraft, fundamentalism can be considered *dangerous* for some democratic societies because wild speculations and uncontrolled experiences pass for unquestioned truth; it misrepresents the scientific attitude by faking the nature of scientific research, by manipulating data, and by selling myth in wrappings that seem scientific (e.g., the Shroud of Turin).[21]

That every man has the right of free speech is truly one of the principles of democracy. This principle can favor the rise of garrulity and it degenerates into demagoguery. Against both there is only one effective weapon: the strength of reason. But philosophical and scientific criticism can do little to erode the great social influence of fundamentalism supported by powerful pressure groups—sometimes entire churches and political parties—by the sympathy of the mass media and, particularly, by popular gullibility. Nevertheless, at least it may be expected to be of some use to give a rational explanation of evolutionary stages of religions. Our present explanation of the *dilemma of fundamentalism* cannot be changed by brute force or by revelation, but can be modified as a result of scientific research, proof, argument, and refutation. That is the great long-term advantage of the scientific outlook: the strength of reason increases its force, without violating the principle of democracy. On the contrary, the main disfunction of fundamentalism is based upon this premise: *it needs belief in order not to understand* and, therefore, must resort to force and social pressure to strengthen its decrepit traditions. In doing so, instead of serving as its basis, democracy vanishes.

NOTES

1. *El animal divino (The Divine Virago), Pentalfa Ed. Oviedo, 1985, 309 pp.*
2. *Cf.* Jeffrey Saver: "An Interview with E. O. Wilson on Sociobiology and Religion," *Free Inquiry* 5, no. 2 (Spring, 1985): pp. 14–22.
3. E. O. Wilson: *On Human Nature* (Cambridge, Mass.: Harvard University Press, 1978), p. 192.

4. *Cf.* "An Interview with E. O. Wilson. . ." *op. cit.* p. 17.

5. For a major overview of his research and his inquiring strategy see, Marvin Harris, *Cultural Materialism* (New York: Random House, Inc., 1979). See also his early work: *The Nature of Cultural Things* (New York: Random House, 1964); and his best-seller: *Cannibals and Kings: The Origins of Cultures,* (New York: Random House, 1977).

6. *Culture, People, Nature,* (New York: Harper and Row, 1980).

7. "Cultural Materialism: Alarms and Excursions," *Behavior Research,* (1985).

8. It is a question widely discussed by historians. See W. Nestle, *Vom Mythos zum Logos. Die Selbstentfaltung des grichischen Denkens von Homer bis auf die Sophistik und Sokrates* (Stuttgart, 1942); J. Burnet, *Early Greek Philosophy,* 3d ed., (London, 1920); B. Snell, *Die Entdeckung des Geistes,* Hamburgo (Eng. trans. *The Discovery of the Mind* [Oxford, 1953]): F. M. Cornford, *From Religion to Philosophy. A Study in the Origin of Western Speculation* (London, 1912); F. M. Cornford, *Principium sapientae. The Origins of Greek Philosophical Thought* (Cambridge University Press, 1925); W. Jaeger, *The Theology of the Early Greek Philosophers,* (Oxford, 1947); P. M. Schuyhl, *Essai sur la formation de la pensée grecque. Introduction historique à une étude de la philosophie platonicienne,* 2d ed., (Paris, 1949), J. P. Vernant, *Mythe et pensée chez les grec,* (Paris, 1965); etc.

9. *Vom Ursprung und Ziel der Geschichte* (Zürich, 1949).

10. *Cf. Science in History* (London: C. A. Watts and Co. Ltd., London, 1964).

11. *Cannibals and Kings, op. cit.* cap. 12.

12. *El animal divino, op. cit.* p. 264.

13. Ibid.

14. Peter Singer, *Animal Liberation.* (New York 1975); Peter Singer and Tom Regan (eds.) *Animal Rights and Human Obligations* (Englewood Cliffs, N.J., 1976).

15. *El animal divino, op. cit.,* p. 280. It is clear that this interpretation is only applicable, while the appearances of interplanetary visitors are imaginative, not real. In any case Gustavo Bueno adds: "Let's consider as a formal merit of our theory of the stages of religion, its potentiality for self-readjustment in accordance with the possible *effective facts* which could happen (for instance, the visit of *extraterrestrial beings*). In line with that, the stages instituted do not mark *a priori* a future arrangement, in any case unverifiable, but subordinates their arrangement to the facts, even though offering categories for locating them in a unitarian frame. And, if fortuitously the *extraterrestrial beings* would visit the earth in five centuries, for instance, only then would be talk of return toward the *primary ligament* and, so much better, towards the *natural ligament* in a new feature." *El animal divino,* p. 305.

16. *Cf.* A classical instance of the dispute between theism and materialism in W. James: *The Will to Believe and Other Essays* (New York, London, 1897) and *The Varieties of Religious Experience* (New York, London, 1902).

17. Carl F. H. Henry, "Religious Liberty: Cornerstone of Human Rights," *Free Inquiry* 4, no. 2 (Spring, 1984): p. 14.

18. Paul Kurtz, "Democracy Without Theology," *Free Inquiry* 4, no. 2, (Spring, 1984): p. 27.

19. Ibid.

20. See on this crucial epistemological issue the of Mario Bunge against the methodological anarchism of P. K. Feyerabend: "Demarcating Science from Pseudoscience," *Fundamenta Scientae,* 3; *Seudosciencia e ideologfa,* Alianza, Madrid, 1985, etc.

21. *Cf.* Joe Nickell, *Inquest on the Shroud of Turin* (Buffalo, N.Y.: Prometheus Books, 1983); "Update on the Shroud of Turin," *Free Inquiry* 5, no. 2 (Spring, 1985).

Communist-Fundamentalist and Liberal-Democratic Ideology

Svetozar Stojanović

WHAT IS IDEOLOGY?

Marx's notion of ideology has been systematically recon-
structed in literature many times; thus I would like to make
only two points. Sometimes he understands ideology as the
idealistic illusion of self-movement in the world of ideas. This
refers to the notion entertained by thinkers, scientists, and
politicans that the only genuine impetus for creating and
explaining new ideas lies in (existing) ideas. Marx also uses
the concept of ideology in another, much more specific way,
and, even today, the theory and study of ideology cannot
be developed without taking it into account: ideology is a
set of ideas that *conceal separate, especially class interests,*
presenting them as meta-historical, that is, as God-given,
natural, universal, rational, and the like. I will be capitalizing
on this meaning.

In my opinion, ideology should be defined as a *set of
ideas that social groups use, at the expense of truth, to justify
or discredit a social order or the forces opposing it.* Thus, both
justifying and discrediting an existing order—but also the power
that, according to these ideas, should replace it—can have an
ideological character. Since Marxism emerged as a critique of

a given (capitalist) order, Marxists in their definitions of ideology often overlook this function of *discrediting the existing system of power* and *justifying the new one* as advocated by the said ideology. Conservatives, on the other hand, try to disqualify as ideological all ideas that question the status quo and recommend a new social order. My definition avoids this trap as well, because discrediting forces opposed to the existing order can also have ideological features. Finally, my definition leaves room for not only the ideology of those in power and those aspiring to power, but also of those who rationalize their subordinate position.

Anthony Giddens recently came out with several interesting theses on ideology. He, too, defines ideology by means of power, but, unlike me, he denies the need to understand it in contrast to truth. First he says: "I want to reject the idea that ideology can be defined in reference to truth claims" (thesis I). Then he claims (thesis II) that the sanctioning of systems of domination suffices as a definition: "Drawing upon this second Marxian strand [which ties ideology with the problem of domination], I therefore propose to interpret the concept of ideology in the following way. *I want to define ideology as the mode in which forms of signification are incorporated within systems of domination so as to sanction their continuance.* I take it to be the typical case of such a notion of ideology that sectional interests are represented as universal interests. This is the basic mode in which forms of signification are incorporated within systems of domination in class societies."[1]

I want to start by making a less important objection to the second thesis, and then move on to cast a critical eye on the first. There is absolutely no reason that we should limit ideology, like Giddens, to *sanctioning* systems of domination, when *discrediting* them can have similar ideological characteristics.

Also, for Giddens the concept of "ideology" is critical rather than neutral. It is, however, unclear how a critique of ideology can avoid arbitrariness and relativism if it does not contrast them with truth. Here is an illustration. Let's imagine a society that is attacked from without and can defend itself only if it is strictly hierarchically organized. Can we assess the justification of this order of power as ideological in the same (critical) sense that we would assess it if it were allegedly based on "God-given" or "natural" human inequality? After all, in the said definition, Giddens himself says that in "basic" ideological cases "sectional interests are represented as universal interests." But, doesn't this mean that ideologies *untruthfully* present systems of domination? And how is this to be dovetailed with his first thesis?

When using the notion of untruth ("at the expense of truth") to define ideology, I, to be sure, do not mean any naive objectivistic, and still less absolutist notion of truth. I agree with Richard Bernstein: "I do not think that there are any fixed criteria by which we can, once and for all, distinguish 'false consciousness' from 'true consciousness.' The achievement of 'true consciousness' is a regulative ideal of the critique of ideology. . . . This does not mean that we must remain intellectually agnostic, that we are never in a position to evaluate and judge the ways in which an ideology is systematically distortive and reflects reified powers of domination. We can show the falsity of an ideology without claiming that we have achieved a final, absolute, 'true' understanding of social and political reality."[2]

There are countless ways in which ideologies try, *at the expense of truth,* to justify or discredit orders of power or the forces opposing them. Only one of them consists of presenting special interests as universal interests. And there are even completely opposite cases: Nazi ideology, for instance, often attacked conceptions and ideologies referring to universal human interests, and it did so explicitly in the name of special racial and national interests. Since Marx's criticism focused mostly on bourgeois-democratic ideology, which belongs to the family of ideologies having universal-humanistic claims, many Marxists under his influence unjustifiably define all ideologies as sets of ideas by which special interests are disguised as universal interests.

My definition of ideology, like any other, can determine only the primary function: justification or discrediting of social orders. Examples of secondary and derivative functions would include, for instance, stabilization-destabilization or integration-disintegration. It may be superfluous to say that justification-discrediting need not at all be direct and open, but rather can be carried out by diverting attention from or covering up what cannot be justified-discredited, by overemphasis on positive or negative aspects, etc.

Those who *define* ideology as "distorted" or "false" consciousness forget that there are many forms of "distorted" or "false" consciousness that have no ideological character at all. In doing so, they assess a kind of consciousness before anything is said about its properties and functions. *Distorted, false,* and (I have suggested) *lying* consciousness are, in my opinion, dominant dimensions of ideologies, or phases in their transformation.

Ideology as "distorted" consciousness is a mixture of truths and untruths, and as "false" consciousness it is a set of untruths. The difference between "false" and "lying" consciousness is that in the first case the proponents of ideology are not conscious of its untruthfulness, whereas in the second case they are. Ideologies usually emerge in history as "distorted" consciousness. With time, as they exhaust themselves, they increasingly try to defend themselves *consciously* at the expense of truth.

It may seem to the casual reader that my suggestion

of "lying consciousness" merely constitutes a return to the Enlightenment's obsolete approach to ideology. As is known, the great thinkers of the Enlightenment interpreted and rejected dominant medieval ideas as conscious deception in the service of rulers and the church. This was too simplified a view for Marx and Engels. They spoke about "distorted" or "false," but not "lying" consciousness.

However, history of philosophy and social thought shows how conceptions that appear to have been buried forever often reemerge, albeit with important modifications and much more limited significance. It is my opinion that this is the case with the Enlightenment's concept of ideology. *Sometimes, ideologies predominantly use conscious lies.* I am sure, for instance, that Goebbels and his apparatus knew very well they were lying in their ideological propaganda. This is why we should adopt the Enlightenment's insight about "lying" consciousness—but at the same time it should be limited to a dimension or stage of some ideologies. In the following passage Marx is coming very close to that:

> The more the normal form of intercourse of society, and with it the conditions of the ruling class, develop their contradiction to the advanced productive forces, and the greater the consequent discord within the ruling class itself as well as between it and the class ruled by it, the more fictitious, of course, becomes the consciousness which originally corresponded to this form of intercourse (i.e., it ceases to be the consciousness corresponding to this form of intercourse), and the more do the old traditional ideas of these relations of intercourse, in which actual private interests, etc., etc., are expressed as universal interests, descend to the level of mere idealizing phrases, conscious illusions, deliberate hypocrisy.[3]

One reason this idea was not expressed in Marx's conception of ideology would seem to be that he concentrated on analyzing and criticizing the bourgeois ideology of his day and age, which can freely be described as "distorted," although certainly not as "lying" consciousness. Anyway, that was a time when progress in understanding the ideological phenomenon truly required distancing oneself as far as possible from the Enlightenment's oversimplifications.

WHAT SHOULD IDEAL-LOGY BE?

I think another notion for a dimension or phase of ideology should be introduced—ideal-logy.[4] I define it as follows: *ideal-logy is a set of ideals that social groups use, at the expense of truth, to justify or discredit a social order or the forces opposing it.* Tying up ideal-logy with untruth ("at the expense of truth") provides for the distinction between the nonideological formulation and justification of ideals on the one hand, and ideal-logy, on the other hand.

But ideals cannot be distorted or false in the epistemological sense of the words. And yet, this dimension or phase of ideology is also characterized by subordinating and sacrificing truth to the requirements of justification or discrediting. The principal modes of ideal-logical (self) delusion are yet to be systematically studied.

In ideal-logy, untruth (partial or complete) often comes to expression in comprehending the relationship between means and ends, especially the ultimate ends (ideals). Ideal-logies most often set social goals, and only then seek out suitable means to realize them. Languages often reflect this ideal-logical temptation. In English there is no *one single* word that focuses our attention on the adequacy of the end to the *available* means. Similarly, no *one single* word designates the adequacy of the means to the sought end.

With their ideal-logies, social groups often delude themselves and others as to the realizability of their goals and ideals, the nature of the means they use, and in terms of believing that they can realize their declared goals and ideals through *these* means. How else can one fully understand and analyze futuristic ideologies, especially radical ones. Even important intellectuals can long be the victims of an ideal-logical approach to reality. The history of communist and other parties is full of such examples.

In ideal-logies the nature of the means looks as though it is strongly determined by the ends, even the most distant, whereas in reality the relationship between ends and means is most often the other way round. Unlike social ends, social means exist *also* outside the consciousness of the actor (individual and collective) and so, in the long run and ultimately, they as a rule are ontologically superior to ends, especially the supreme ends. It is no wonder that political activity so often witnesses an inversion of ends and means: the latter become ends unto themselves and the former serve as their ideal-logical justification.

Revolutionary ideologies counter the existing order with an ideal of a different social system. It is in this predominant form—of ideal-logy—that bourgeois democratic ideology appeared on the historical stage. This is how communist ideology also embarked on its road.

Ideologies most often begin their life as ideal-logies, and then more and more are transformed into some kind of real-logies. It is a term that I am proposing to designate a special dimension or phase of ideology. I have in mind a continuum with ideal-logy and real-logy at its opposite ends. In order to justify a social order (or forces opposing it), *real-logy no longer refers to ideals, but rather to "realization" and the principle of "realism."*

Bourgeois-democratic ideology in some interpretations has traversed the road from conceiving democracy as the "rule of the people" to actually reducing it to pluralism and competition among political elites for power. This real-logy has brought about a certain de-ideologi⁻ᵗion of bourgeois democracy. However, at the same time it has been proclaimed as not only the greatest achievement in the development of democracy to date, but also as its ultimate possible achievement—and this, again, is ideological (self) delusion. Surprisingly, no one has terminologically captured this negative legitimization in contrast to "real socialism": *real democracy,* allegedly, can only be the circulation of ruling political elites by means of free elections and can succeed only in capitalism. Bolshevism has also gone through an ideal-logical phase primarily invoking the ideal of a classless and stateless society.

ERRONEOUS GENERALIZATIONS

The history of the twentieth century has been strongly marked by the clash between two major ideologies: communist and bourgeois-democratic. Their *structural tendencies* are very different, and even contrary to one another. That is why any attempt to take one or the other type of ideology as a model for generalizing and defining ideology leads one astray. Let me illustrate this by two unsuccessful attempts, one from the anti-Marxist and the other from the Marxist circle.

Karl Dietrich Bracher, the West German historian and theoretician, takes the following approach to ideology:

The character and workings of modern ideologies can best be seen in the sharpest, most exclusive form, which emerges

*when totalitarian political objectives and styles of thought
step onto the scene.* The essence and function of ideologi-
zation in the state and society are especially reflected in
totalitarian views of the world, whether we ascribe them
to older strata of monocratic thought or extract them from
Rousseauism and the radical egalitarianism of the French
Revolution, or want to ascribe them only to the left-radical
and right-radical extremism of socialism and national-so-
cialism in our century.

The nucleus of this process is the tendency to over-
simplify complex realities: the striving to reduce them to
a *single* truth and at the same time to dichotomize them
into good and bad, right and wrong, friend and foe, to
view the world in a bipolar way on the basis of a single
model of explanation. Marxist class and national-socialist
racial theory are two cases in point. Building stereotypes
of the enemy and a strategy for seeking out the sacrificial
lamb as a means to simplify and integrate social and political
plurality is as important as are vague promises and visions. . . . Guarantees of absolute truth, not just in heaven
but here on earth, give ideology the character of a secularized
religion of salvation and atonement.[5]

Like Bracher, many Western analysts and critics of ideology
have been so "impressed" by the "totalitarian" kind of
ideologies (national-socialist and Stalinist) that they have
proclaimed their properties as universal. Hardly anything of
what we quoted from Bracher can be applied, for instance,
to bourgeois-democratic ideology. Is not the designation
"ideology" itself ideologically highly biased when it does not
also embrace this major and still very powerful ideological
complex.

All the features that Bracher sees as the defining characteristics of ideology, are for Agnes Heller signs that this
is not a question of ideology in the true sense of the word.
In her opinion, *every* ideology claims to "represent the cause
of the whole of mankind," yet despite this universalistic

pretension it "only generalizes class-specific, i.e., particular interests."[6] Such a restrictive definition was bound to lead to an unacceptable conclusion: "According to this definition we reach the conclusion, which may sound bold, that in the case of so-called Soviet ideology it is not really a question of ideology at all."[7] And, why is this alleged "Soviet ideology" not to be really included in ideologies, but only in "state doctrines" and "systems of dogmas"? Heller gives three reasons:

First, ideology (according to the above definition) pretends to express universal interests (and in fact it expresses class interests) whereas "Soviet ideology" claims to represent class (proletarian) interests. However, we have already established that there are other ideologies that also do not pretend to express universal interests.

Second, "Ideologies in the above sense compete, emerge on the market, always see themsevles as a part of plurality. Marxism-Leninism, on the other hand, does not join any race, it excludes all other ideologies. And thereby it ceases to be an ideology in the real sense of the word."[8] The very mention of competition in the market shows that it is the liberal ideology that here serves as a model for definition. Thus the ideological field is further narrowed down: not a single state-monopolistic ideology—and they unquestionably account for the majority, both in the past and today—is really an ideology.

Third, the soviet "state doctrine" is not concerned with its own coherence since, like a creed, it is not subject to criticism. This introduces yet another, this time rationalistic-logical narrowing down of the concept of ideology. The result? The vast majority of past and present ideologies could not be encompassed by this concept.

Heller adds that she does not believe that "there has never been ideology in Soviet-type societies." She claims it took a long time to transform "Marxist ideology" into "state doctrine." It was not until around 1922 that non-Marxist theories started being banned. For a while members of the "party aristocracy" had an equal right to take part in debates on the common theoretical heritage, and in mutual discussions they still, for a while, used rational arguments. Later, Marxism became illegal precisely because, with its "ideological character," it allowed and brought a certain "theoretical pluralism."

Thus, it would turn out that only non-state *ideology* exists in "Soviet-type societies"; that Leninism is ideology, but Stalinism is not; that, for instance, somebody like Lukacs is an ideologist, but Stalin is not. I would like to point out, however, that I have only criticized Heller's definition of ideology and its consequences, and not other aspects of her analysis of the "Soviet state doctrine."

LIBERAL-DEMOCRATIC AND STATE-MONOPOLISTIC IDEOLOGY

Bourgeois ideology, both in its economic-liberal and in its political-democratic form, draws and *limits* the attention to what is evident: equal rights, elections, political pluralism, and so on. Since it is largely rooted in everyday experience,[9] this ideology is "capillary" in the way it spreads and has a great magnetic power. One might almost say: by its very force, spontaneously, that which strikes the eye—here creates its own justification. However, in directing human consciousness to immediate reality, this ideology also conceals the mechanisms of class domination.

No one has to work hard to hide them: they are *structurally* concealed. Namely, the separation of "civil society" and the state opens room for legal and political freedom and equality, as well as democracy, and at the same time makes the class domination, which is carried over from the economy into other spheres of social life and power, hardly visible.

Hence, it is perfectly understandable that the bourgeoisie (as the non-ruling dominant class) should have incomparably less of a need to engage in centralized ideological production and indoctrination than the statist (ruling) class—although at first glance we might expect it to be the other way round, because the statist class, in addition to its ideological monopoly, can, if it deems it necessary, also use its monopoly over state repression.

Marxists who have forgotten the separation of "civil society" and the state under capitalism overlook the fact that bourgeois ideologies are emerging, spreading, and operating primarily in the sphere of "civil society." Just as the birthplace of the dominant class in capitalism is in this sphere, and not in the state apparatus, so it is also the birthplace of bourgeois ideologies.

This is not to say that Antonio Gramsci erred when he stressed the role of intellectuals and the ideological apparati (educational institutions, the mass media, etc.) in capitalism. But, "ideological apparati" and "ideological state apparati" (Louis Althusser's expression) are not the same thing. It is absurd, as Althusser does, to treat the family, the entire school system, the church, and all mass media as ideological *state* apparati. In capitalism not even political parties are state but rather private organizations.

However, even if we were to apply the notion of "ideological state apparatus" properly, we could not ascribe to it such an immense, and still less a central, role in creating and spreading bourgeois ideologies, simply because they originate in "civil society" rather than in the state apparatus. In overlooking the separation of "civil society" from the state in capitalism, it appears that Althusser unconsciously projected into this state the place and function of ideology in a typical ruling communist party (here the category of ideological *party-state* apparatus would fit). Anyone who sets out from the way in which ideology is created and spread in countries where communist parties are in power, and then applies that model to the West, will never really grasp how ideology emerges and spreads in capitalism.

To be sure, liberal and democratic bourgeois ideology has the form not only of the everyday and spontaneous consciousness of the "ordinary" man, but also of "high" ideology. Since in terms of content there is a homology between these two ideological levels, the latter falls on the fertile ground of the former. Of course, the former is fragmented, incoherent and sometimes even chaotic. However, one cannot talk about "introduction of consciousness from outside," but rather about systematization, elaboration, and justification of the existing consciousness. The dominant class of "civil society" in capitalism has as a rule no "vanguard party" that pretends to interpret and represent its "objective interests."

It is an entirely different matter when we talk about an ideology whose basic statements, according to the Bolshevik idea, are created outside of everyday and spontaneous consciousness of the working class, and need to be *introduced into it from outside,* even despite its *resistance.* It is not surprising, therefore, that Bolshevik-oriented communists in the West have never fully understood why liberal and democratic ideology has a much greater influence over "ordinary" people, and even workers, than their ideology of the "objective interests" of those same people and workers. The Bolshevik approach is fundamentally wrong, because it postulates that liberal and democratic ideology must also be introduced in the working class from outside.

Practically all the basic differences between these two
types of ideologies can be expressed by the image of market
competition on the one side, and monopoly on the other.
Market competition and selection is said to be the basic
mechanism regulating relations between the economic, political and ideological contestants in capitalism. State-
monopoly ideology, of course, does not allow the market
of ideas. Free supply and demand may eventually exist
regarding material goods, but absolutely not regarding spiritual products, especially those of key importance to ideological control. On part of the Leftist intelligentsia, with its
sweeping, *undifferentiated* attack on "the market in culture,"
has unwittingly helped to suppress the autonomy of intellectual
work in statism.

An ideology in which all (even merely potential) com-
petitors are declared enemies suits a centrally planned,
distributive, and command economy. This is a question of
the Manichaean polarization of the world. A kind of almost
permanent "war communism" is marked by an irreconcilable
"ideological *struggle.*" This is a language overflowing with
wartime metaphors: front, battlefield, battle, and the like. It
takes a lot of time, social resistance and crisis before the
"vanguard" realizes that, with no major threat to itself, the
slogan "Who isn't with us is against us" can be replaced with
the slogan "Who isn't against us is with us."

This Manichaean mentality has carried over to emigrants
as well. Here is what one of them, Andrei Sinyavski, said
in an interview (to the West German weekly *Die Zeit* on
October 19, 1984):

> Roughly and schematically speaking, one can now
> distinguish between an authoritarian-nationalistic and
> liberal-democratic wing of Russian emigre dissidents. The
> leader of the first group, which is supported by the majority
> of Russian emigrants, is Alexander Solzhenyitsin. I count

myself in the second group. . . .

The gap between those in Russia who think differently is traditionally deep. For us someone who thinks differently than we do is our enemy. In Soviet Russia they call him the enemy, "the agent of imperialism"; here they call him "the agent of the KGB." The Soviet authorities have drummed into our heads a vision of omnipresent enemies, enemies, enemies against whom we must fight, fight, fight.

Characteristic of *liberal and democratic ideology* is that it allows legal activity by every group and party that respects the state constitution. Some other ideologies in capitalist countries (under certain conditions even the dominant ideology) often have structural tendencies that are very similar to the dictatorial-statist ideology. Suffice it to recall the Manichaeism of McCarthyism or the current fundamentalism of the "moral majority" in the United States, which is obsessed with both the "communist threat," and the fear of a liberal attitude to the "communist enemy."

The image of an open *or* occupied space can also help us to compare the two ideologies. The market suggests the image of a space accessible to everyone in principle. State monopoly ideology, on the other hand, has a need to homogenize and fill in the ideological space. As soon as a crack appears, ideological guardians rush to eliminate all "foreign" ideas. They are panic-stricken by the "empty space the enemy can use." Without this striving for totality one cannot understand the big *surplus of ideology in statism*. Because of the growing *ennui* it produces, this kind of "Marxism" becomes increasingly repugnant.

While the liberal-democratic ideology is characterized by its abstraction from differences (the principle of equalization), by blunting the blade of conflicts and by neutralization— dictatorial-statist ideology aggravates conflicts and demands universal allegiance to the party in the name of science.

Marxist-Leninist ideology has also proclaimed itself a science. Lenin himself took pride in "scientific ideology." This ideological monopoly implicitly justifies itself by claiming that its challengers would ultimately have to be "laymen" who have no place in a "scientific" debate. There is a kind of "scientific" monopoly also over definitions: they are seen as empirical statements, even scientific laws, not as stipulations by ideological powerholders.

There has long been a separate discipline in the Soviet Union, which is studied and taught at all levels: it is called "scientific communism." I would say it is a kind of "science fiction." From its emergence to the present phase of "real socialism," this ideology has faced almost insurmountable obstacles in understanding real capitalism. Since the social sciences and philosophy in the USSR are not free, the "Soviet" understanding of the West depends much more on the interests, experience, and mentality of its own leaders than is the case with the Western understanding of the USSR.

It would be very important to study the hermeneutic aspects in these two ideologies' confrontation: the liberal-democratic and the state-monopolistic. There is a whole range of self-projections that impede them from properly understanding each other. An analysis of this social-psychological mechanism could, in my opinion, open up major prospects for a comparative study of ideologies.

What primarily interests me here is the fact that a ruling (statist) class projects its power structure onto a capitalist system where there is no ruling, but only a dominant class. It is no wonder, then, that statist ideologists should misapprehend the dominant ideology in capitalism. These two mutually opposed ideologies function, spread, and gain influence in entirely different ways. Here we are dealing with social totalities of which the one is dominated by *monopoly politics* and the other by *competitive economics*.

It is extremely hard for an ideology marked by monism, monopoly of the party-state apparatus, monological structure, scientific-nomological pretensions, and repression, to fathom the ideology of pluralism, the circulation of elites in governing the state, dialogue, the separation of science from ideology, social contract, and tolerance.

ON HERBERT MARCUSE'S CRITIQUE OF "REPRESSIVE TOLERANCE"

Marcuse concentrates[10] on analyzing the historical development of tolerance: from liberating tolerance at the beginning of modern times to the present day.[11] He says that tolerance is an integral part of the ruling ideology, because it obliges respect for the rules of hierarchically structured power. To put it ironically: it is slightly harder for those at the bottom to tolerate those at the top of the hierarchy of power, than the other way round. Delving through the veil of abstract ideas-values, Marcuse tries to reach the source of concrete power and discover the "background limitations." His findings: what seems like unbiased tolerance actually shields the "established machinery of discrimination" and suits conservative views and movements, discriminating against all Leftist and generally progressive social forces.

Marcuse's formula of "repressive tolerance" calls attention to the need to examine the ways in which tolerance is transformed into the ideology of domination. Such formulas are suitable for heuristic purposes, because they draw attention to the limitations in realizing values and even to the functional transformation into their own opposite. In such a case one should call it: the *negative dialectics of tolerance*.

The trouble does not start until such *initial heuristic moves*

are seen as final theoretical categories. Marcuse should have
drawn a sharper line between tolerance and repression, rather
than almost erasing it with the notion of repressive tolerance.
As a result, unfortunately, he played into the hands of
ideologizers of his own theory. This example shows the major
role language plays in creating the ideological potential of
theory. The notion of *manipulative tolerance,* in my view,
would have been much less open to the danger of ideolog-
ization than the concept of "repressive tolerance."

There have been Leftists who turn Marcuse's critique
of the "ideology of tolerance" into an *ideology of "repressive
tolerance."* Proceeding from the correct premise that differences between democracy and dictatorship in capitalism are
not absolute, they draw the wrong and very dangerous
conclusion that these differences are negligible. This is one
of the countless variations on the claim that the difference
between tolerance and democracy on the one hand, and
repression and dictatorship on the other, is only *formal* in
character, whereas in *essence* in both cases it is a matter of
the dictatorship of the ruling class.

What, according to Marcuse, is repressive tolerance to
be replaced by? Selective intolerance: expanding tolerance for
ideas and movements on the Left, and intolerance for those
on the Right. He goes so far as to recommend not only
"the withdrawal of toleration of speech and assembly from
groups and movements which promote aggressive policies,
armament, chauvinism, discrimination on the grounds of race
and religion," but also from those "which oppose the extension
of public services, social security, medical care, etc.," and
generally the established universe of discourse and behavior—
thereby precluding *a priori* a rational evaluation of the
alternatives.[12]

The scope of intolerance is thereby extended to "the stage
of action as well as of discussion and propaganda, of deed

as well as of word."[13] Marcuse feels, of course, that the following two questions are of crucial importance here. First, does an *objective criterion* exist to differentiate what should from what should not be tolerated? Second, *who* is competent to apply such a criterion?

He says this criterion consists of "reasonable chance for pacification and liberation." A "historical calculus of progress" is possible that should be based on rationally comparing the consequences of maintaining the existing state with the consequences of supporting the alternative. Unfortunately, Marcuse does not analyze the historical experience, which shows that movements that substantially restrict freedom of speech, assembly, and activity seldom lead to "pacification and liberation." Does not the rational basis for assessing what we can expect from a victorious social movement include its attitude—be it guardian or destructive—toward the scope already won for democracy and tolerance?

Marcuse's answer as to who is competent to make the assessment is equally poor: "Everyone 'in the maturity of his faculties' as a human being, everyone who has learned to think rationally and autonomously. The answer to Plato's educational dictatorship is the *democratic educational dictatorship of free men.*"[14] The answer only multiplies the problems. Who should separate those with "mature faculties," who think "rationally and autonomously," who are thus "free"—from other people, and how? How could one prevent what happens so often, i.e., dictatorship in the name of freedom turning into dictatorshp against freedom? Finally, what does "democratic educational dictatorship of free men" really mean? What would it roughly look like? How would it be introduced? What strikes the eye is that Marcuse's idea is even more vague than Marx's notion of the dictatorship of the proletariat.

Marcuse says not a word about these key questions in this essay or in few of his other writings.[15] I have to say that he (in spite of his unquestionable contributions to the development of humanistic Marxism), having facilely launched the idea of "the democratic educational dictatorship of free men," laid the foundation for the possible ideological abuse of his own conception. In this context Marcuse's negative stand on dictatorial communism is not much help:

> The factual barriers which totalitarian democracy erects against the efficacy of qualitative dissent are weak and pleasant enough compared with the practices of a dictatorship which claims to educate the people in the truth. With all its limitations and distortions, democratic tolerance is under all circumstances more humane than an institutional intolerance which sacrifices the rights and liberties of the living generations for the sake of future generations.[16]

Marcuse does not even raise the question of how to avoid the danger of his "democratic educational dictatorship of free men" being deformed into such a dictatorship. He seems to have realized the difficulties, and only three years later, in a Postscriptum in 1968, said something that is rather different:

> However, the alternative to the establshed semi-democratic process is *not* a dictatorship or elite, no matter how intellectual and intelligent, but the struggle for a real democracy.[17]

But Marcuse's attitude toward democracy in highly developed capitalist states remains highly ambivalent. He criticizes this democracy as "totalitarian" and as a "tyranny of the majority," but also as the class rule of the bourgeoisie. However, if the bourgeoisie rules, there cannot be genuine, but only seeming tyranny of the *majority*. Here is further proof of Marcuse's ambivalence:

The exercise of political rights (such as voting, letter-writing to the press, to Senators, etc., protest-demonstrations with a priori renunciation of counter-violence) in a society of total administration serves to strengthen this administration by testifying to the *existence of democratic liberties which, in reality, have changed their content and lost effectiveness.* In such a case, freedom (of opinion, of assembly, of speech) becomes an instrument for absolving servitude. And yet . . . the *existence and practice of these liberties remain a precondition for the restoration of their original oppositional function,* provided that the effort to transcend their (often self-imposed) limitations is intensified."[18]

But, how can something that has already lost its effectiveness be the precondition for any kind of new effectiveness? One gets the impression that Marcuse, like many other Marxists, often does not know what to do with democracy in capitalism.

Two basic experiences lie at the root of Marcuse's reaction to the social situation. They are "totalitarianism" (both in its Nazi and in its Stalinist version) and American democracy (with its phobia of any kind of socialism). It is interesting to note that the Nazi abuse of democracy prompted Karl Popper to draw the conclusion opposite to that of Marcuse. I am referring to Popper's conclusion based on the paradox of tolerance: an order that cultivates *unlimited* tolerance will probably be destroyed by intolerant groups and movements. That is why he recommended that the instigation of intolerance ought to be a crime.[19]

Marcuse's advocacy of a "democratic educational dictatorship of free men" is, in my view, unacceptable not only to liberals, but also to democratic socialists. In democratic capitalism the only successful Leftist parties are those whose members fight to expand tolerance, not to introduce selective intolerance.

116   Neo-Fundamentalism

NOTES

1. "Four Theses on Ideology," *Canadian Journal of Political and Social Theory* 6, nos. 1–2 (1983): 18–21, emphasis mine.

2. *The Restructuring of Social and Political Theory* (New York: Harcourt Brace Jovanovich, 1976), p. 108.

3. *The German Ideology, Collected Works* (New York. Vol. 5), p. 293.

4. I first used this term in the book *Geschichte und Parteibewusstein* (Munchen, 1978), p. 142. An English translation was published by Prometheus Books, Buffalo, 1981, under the title *In Search of Democracy in Socialism.*

5. *Zeit der Ideologien* (Stuttgart, 1982), p. 16f, emphasis mine.

6. A. Heller, F. Feher, and G. Markus, "Der sowjetische Weg. Bedürfnisdiktatur und entfremdeter Alltag," VSA, 1983, p. 217).

7. Ibid.

8. Ibid., p. 218.

9. *Everyday consciousness* is its principal and most powerful form. Consequently, a critique of bourgeois democracy must primarily be a critique of consciousness in everyday life. Unfortunately, Marx does not not designate as ideological a single form of everyday consciousness.

10. In his essay "On Repressive Tolerance," in R. P. Wolff, B. Moore Jr., and H. Marcuse: *A Critique of Pure Tolerance* (Boston: Beacon Press, 1965).

11. Sometimes one gets the impression that Marcuse compares the ideal(-logy) of tolerance in the early development of capitalism with the practical fate of tolerance in more recent times. It is not true, however, that there was more tolerance earlier in capitalism: the right to vote was very limited at the time, political and trade union organizations of workers were not allowed, etc.

12. Ibid., p. 100f.

13. Ibid., p. 109.

14. Ibid., p. 106, emphasis mine.

15. Unfortunately, Marcus remained too much in the abstract frameworks of philosophy as philosophy to be able to devote serious attention to these problems.

16. Op. cit., p. 99.

17. Ibid., p. 122f.

18. Ibid., p. 84, emphasis mine.

19. *The Open Society and Its Enemies,* Vol. 1, p. 265.

Why Fundamentalism Flourishes

G. A. Wells

Fundamentalists cannot avoid the implications of holding by any sacred book, be it the Bible, the Koran or *Das Kapital.* The book requires interpretation; the interpreters cannot agree on what constitutes the correct interpretation; and so any person or group that cares to pose as an authority declares that theirs is the exposition that must be unquestioningly accepted. And authoritative ruling is what many people want. Society could not cohere if all were rebels, and although some educationalists are apt to stress the value of independence and originality, the great majority of people are far better equipped to do things in a traditional manner, to follow a clear lead, rather than take the initiative. In the presence of a forceful leader, an individual who would feel weak when left to his own devices is more confident, braver, and stronger.

That many people are content to believe what they are told is only to be expected from man's social nature. The solitary animal faces the universe alone. His knowledge of the environment is acquired by personal experience through direct contact, and that part of the environment of which he has no direct experience remains unknown to him and without influence on his behavior. But the member of a herd or society has additional resources. By attending to the reactions of other members of the herd, he is able to react

119

indirectly to events that are not accessible to him through his senses. In this way his attention becomes focused more on the action of his fellows and less on the remainder of the environment. Thus, in the case of human societies, whenever an immediate response to the nonhuman elements in the situation is not required, there is a tendency to respond chiefly to the human elements. Instead of forming his own judgment, the individual tries to determine what the prevailing opinion is, and the habit thus developed may easily overwhelm tendencies to independence.

Such conformity in the majority provides the small minority, in whom tendencies to independence are strongly developed, with a motive for dogmatizing. Men who seek power first try to impose certain beliefs, and in doing so they acquire the prestige associated with special knowledge. Fundamentalist groups illustrate the willingness of millions to trust in the authority of individual leaders. The authority of the great fundamentalist evangelists is far greater than that of bishops or other leaders in the institutional church, or of scholars or theologians in liberal Christianity. In the ancient world, with no railways, no press, no regular post, no radio or television, the scope of charismatic preachers was much more limited. Their present-day success in winning followers on a huge scale naturally increases their own confidence, often to the point where they suppose themselves to be really inspired. This conviction of special inspiration does not so readily arise in the minds of men who owe their superior powers to knowledge legitimately acquired; for they know the source and limitations of their capacity, and thus are not so ready to assume the authoritative tone. Furthermore, the active "missionizing" required of the zealous preacher does not really comport with a life spent in study and inquiry. Intellectual processes mediate between instincts, which supply the driving force, and actual behavior. They guide the animal into the type of behavior that seems best suited to satisfy the instinct. But energy is consumed in these intellectual processes, and if they are complex and protracted, the resulting behavior loses much of the energy originally available. Hence we commonly find greater energy in action from persons whose intellectual processes are brief and limited.

There is a further factor. When our ideas about the immediate environment are very incomplete or erroneous, our behavior is likely to be ill-adapted to our needs, so that we expose ourselves to some immediate unpleasantness. But in this way attention is called to our mistake, and we may be led to rectify it. If, for instance, we believe that ether is a good fire-extinguisher, we shall be in for a rude shock when we act on this belief; and if we survive the experience, the belief will not survive with us. On the other hand, any ideas we may have formed about the nature of the universe, or about the distant future or past, are unlikely to lead to any *noticeably* inappropriate reactions on our part. Thus we may well persist in erroneous beliefs of these kinds all our lives without ever experiencing the smallest surprise or disappointment.

This difference is important. It explains why even the most primitive peoples sometimes appear to have made considerable progress in the practical arts while continuing to hold quite groundless beliefs in matters that do not lend themselves to experimental control. It also explains why in our civilized societies people who are highly educated in fields where all theories are subjected to experimental tests can at the same time—to use their own phrase—"believe in the Bible." They have never bothered with critical study of it, for, as I have said, erroneous views on the Bible do not expose them to any obvious unpleasantness. If you try to explain to them the difficulties that lie in the way of accepting any biblical book at its face value, you have to descend into details, and they are convinced that such attention to detail is mere trivial pedantry. The simplest way to avoid confronting difficulties is to keep to generalities. Many people are prepared to believe—have been brought up to believe—that "in some way" or "in some sense" the Bible is God's revelation. And God himself, in such thinking, may be no more than a sort of something somewhere. It is a long way from this attitude to full-blooded fundamentalism, but such an attitude does provide the fundamentalist preacher with the essential basis on which he can build.

These are among what one might call the perennial conditions favoring religious conformity. To understand why it flourishes so much today we have to look at historical developments. The history of the science shows that, in the early days of investigating a particular set of occurrences, it was relatively easy for a pioneer to get his own explanatory theory published in a textbook, but to dislodge that theory and have it replaced by another in standard works of reference was much more difficult. The earlier theory is regarded as established and can be made to yield only to a thorough and soundly-argued alternative. We see much the same in the history of Bible interpretation, with the added complication that established interests are capable of surviving even the best-argued theories. By the time critical study of the Bible began, uncritical acceptance of it had been traditional for 1500 years. And so we find that a recent apologist does not hesitate to defend such acceptance by arguing that "possession is nine-tenths of the law."[1]

I would stress that critical study of the Bible is not an attempt to prove it wrong, any more than literary criticism is a debunking of literature. Criticism is simply the careful examination of the facts to discover what they really teach, and extremely valuable criticism of the Bible has been conducted by many scholars who, so far from being anxious to discredit it, have been professed Christians.

The basic fundamental position that the Bible is totally inerrant is best countered by studying the details that such scholars have assembled. Take for instance the accounts of the same period of Jewish history given on the one hand in the books of Samuel and Kings and on the other in the book of Chronicles. First Kings 15 tells that King Asa "did that which was right in the eyes of the Lord . . . but the high places were not taken away." Second Chronicles 14 sums up the reign of the same monarch by expressly contradicting this, saying: "Asa did that which was good and right in the eyes of the Lord; for he took away the strange altars and high places." Scholars have pointed out that the book of Chronicles was written centuries later than the book of Kings, and that its author could not imagine a good king tolerating the high places (local shrines that rival the later unique shrine or temple at Jerusalem), so he amended the account he found in Kings, and did so in perfectly good faith. We are so often told that either we must allow that a biblical narrative is true, or we must admit that we are calling it a sham, a lie, a fraud, or worse. But there is no reason to believe that the chronicler regarded the earlier account as inspired: he will have found it much more plausible to suppose that the author of the book of Kings had got things a bit wrong than to believe that they could have happened as there described.

This is no isolated instance, for the chronicler systematically revises the narrative of Samuel/Kings, and thus betrays how a biblical writer can be inspired by the conceptions of his own times rather than by God. Unfortunately, few people have the leisure or interest to pursue such detailed arguments, and even if they have, they might not find it easy to be guided to appropriate and informative works of reference on the subject. In the nineteenth century there was much more widespread awareness of biblical criticism because the

exponents of the then novel critical scholarship could not
avoid frequent exchanges with conservative opponents, many
of which attracted very wide attention. Today, critical research is no longer primarily concerned with such questions
as: What are the sources and dates of the various books of
the Bible? How did disparate material come to be unified
in a given book and ascribed to an author who did not in
fact write it? Such matters are now regarded in critical circles
as settled, and the relevant traditional conservative views are
ignored because they are no longer regarded as tenable.
Another reason that contemporary critical theologians (with
a few honorable exceptions) make little attempt to come to
terms with ultra-conservative Christians is that they recognize
fundamentalism as a major source of recruitment to
Christianity, and as far preferable to what they call
"materialistic" atheism. The result of all these factors is that
the general public cannot look to the scholars for adequate
exposure of the claims of fundamentalism.

There are additional factors that have come to favor
fundamentalism within the last thirty or forty years. People
are very suggestible when frightened, and today the individual
finds himself living in an unstable international situation with
terrifying developments in armaments, and so wants a faith
that gives him more than tentative reassurance. People taught
from childhood to regard the Bible with respect or even with
reverence are ready to believe preachers who tell them that
atomic physics has at last confirmed the prophecy of Isaiah—
actually it is pseudo-Isaiah[2]—(ch. 24), "the foundations of
the earth shake, earth breaks to pieces," etc., and that only
those who have faith in the God of the Bible will survive
the imminent catastrophe. The liberal theologian Dr. David
Jenkins has told how disconcerted he was to find, on re-
linquishing his theological chair for appointment as Bishop
of Durham, that what his flock require from him is not the

"exploration, critical re-assessment and discovery," which, as a liberal, he would be happy to provide, but rather "assurance" and "reinforcement in opinions and positions already held."[3] Liberal theology, recognizing as it does difficulties in what has for centuries been taught as Christian doctrine, cannot provide such assurance; its qualifications and hesitations testify only to doubt, and "he that doubteth is like the surge of the sea, driven by the wind and tossed" (James 1:6). The author of this epistle knew—as many have known (they include Nietzsche and Hitler)—that emphatic assertion is often more effective than careful statement of pros and cons; that arguments suggest the possibility of dissenting views, and that to defend one's opinions is to admit that they are open to attack.[4] What is called the old-time Bible faith, promulgated by well-organized groups with massive propaganda, gives certain and unhesitating answers, and is welcomed for that.

Adequate religious education would make a big difference here. I do not believe that what is called "religious education" in schools tells the pupils how the Bible came into existence, how limited is its historical value, and how confused and contradictory are the ethical principles that are proclaimed in its various books. How many schoolchildren learn that the gospels are relatively late documents and therefore more questionable as sources for Christian origins than many of the epistles that view Jesus so differently? How many are aware that the fourth of the canonical gospels is in significant respects incompatible with the other three, or that, in the case of these three, a narrative in Mark is often carefully rewritten by Matthew or Luke so as to make it mean something substantially different? How many know that virgin birth is documented not even in all of these three, but, in the whole of the New Testament, only in the two nativity stories of Matthew and Luke, and that each one of these is incompatible with the other, as well as being full of its own difficulties?[5] Ignorance on these matters persists even though Christian scholars have long since shown that, for instance, the passages in Isaiah, Micah, Hosea, and Jeremiah, to which the author of the gospel of Matthew alludes as prophecies of details of Jesus' infancy, have no real relevance to the episodes in question; that, for instance, it is ridiculous to suppose, as Matthew does in his chapter 2, that Jeremiah 31:15 (Rachel weeping for her children) refers to Herod's slaughter of the Innocents. It is in the interests of all the churches that pupils are not encouraged to be critical about the Bible and are seldom told about the criticisms that have been made in the past. And fundamentalism thrives on the ignorance that results.

Fundamentalists are also able to persuade people that world conditions have become so much worse since 1914 that the end of the world and the final judgment, said in some gospel passages to follow such worsening, cannot now be long delayed. They do not, of course, realize that there is no uniform teaching about the end-times in the Bible, that the apocalyptic discourse on this subject put into Jesus' mouth in the gospel of Mark was rewritten by Luke so as to give a different time-scale.[6] Nor do they realize that apocalypses are characteristically products of times of affliction, that their authors sought to keep alive the hope of the believers by promising deliverance *soon,* and were not in the least concerned with what is to happen thousands of years after their own time. Furthermore, it is not even true that there has been universal unmitigated deterioration since 1914. The First World War was indeed more swiftly destructive of life than its predecessors, but not more brutal, nor more pernicious in its effects than, say, the Thirty Years' War of the seventeenth century, which practically annihilated Germany and prostrated her for generations. Wars notwithstanding, the industrial horrors of the eighteenth and nineteenth centuries and much of the disease, squalor, and poverty that went with life at that time have been abolished in a substantial fraction of the world. Here it is ignorance, not of the Bible but of history, that boosts the religious case. It is precisely because so many men and women are today better fed and less exhausted by their work than ever before that they have energy and leisure to muse on what they call "the human predicament" and to convince themselves that it is hopeless.

Another important factor in the current success of fundamentalism has been the reaction against communism. The odium attaching to communism has been transferred to all criticism of religious belief, since the communists have constituted themselves the official directors of the anti-religious movement and disinterested inquirers are mortified to find themselves in the same camp as Marxist zealots who can be as fanatical as the proponents of any other revelation. We hear much about defending "Christian values" against communism, when in fact communism can be criticized much more effectively on rational than on such religious grounds. The struggle against communist ideology is needlessly handicapped by association of democratic ideals with superstition.

The efficacy of patriotism in promoting fundamentalism (patriotic revulsion against Russian atheism) illustrates that a really far-reaching movement often owes its success to its appeal to a number of basic human tendencies, and not just to one. In Scotland, Northern Ireland, and Wales, a very conservative evangelism is reinforced by strong national feeling. In the case of Wales further reinforcement comes from the ancient musical culture of the country, which provides fervent hymn-singing in the chapels. Two or three factors reinforcing each other are far more potent than one in isolation. As for patriotism, while I accept that any community must be prepared to defend itself against enemies, I also think that our educators need to do more to warn against its negative aspects; for it can all too easily become a way of satisfying and of nourishing one's own importance. Feeling ourselves part of a majestic whole, we have the satisfaction of admiring ourselves.

The great difficulty one has in combating religious ideas is that, as soon as one such idea is discredited, the powerful organizations concerned come up with another. Truth, Anatole France remarked, is one, and this makes it a poor competitor with error. I recall in this connection Robert Louis Stevenson's fable "The House of Eld." The hero belongs to a group who, unlike "the heathen," wears a fetter on the right leg, and deem this indispensable to salvation. He is determined to abolish this ridiculous and burdensome custom, even though his reforming zeal involves him in killing his uncle, his father, and his mother. At least his fellows agree that wearing a fetter on the right leg is a superstition. They explain that the correct doctrine is that it is to be worn on the left leg.

NOTES

1. J. W. Wenham, *Christ and the Bible* (London, 1972), p. 74. I owe this point to James Barr's very useful study *Fundamentalism,* 2d ed., London, 1981, p. 182.

2. The Old Testament scholar H. H. Rowley has noted that the apocalyptic material beginning at chapter 24 is "quite certainly not Isianic" and "totally different in outlook and in spirit from anything else in the book of Isaiah" (*The Growth of the Old Testament,* 3d ed., 1967, p. 89).

3. See Dr. Jenkins's article in the English daily newspaper *The Guardian* (17 February, 1984).

4. See Nietzsche's *Menschliches Allzumenschliches,* Vol. 2, aphorism no. 295; and Hitler's *Mein Kampf,* Vol. 1, ch. 6. Nietzsche was obligatory reading for Nazis because he

opposed egalitarianism and claimed special privileges for the superman. But he was hardly pro-German (he even thought of forming an anti-German league), said next to nothing about Jews, and did not proclaim the inequality of races. For details, see J. R. Baker, *Race* (Oxford University Press, 1974), pp. 44–6, 55–9.

5. For details, see my *The Jesus of the Early Christians,* (London: Pemberton, 1971), chapter 1.

6. For details, see my *The Historical Evidence for Jesus,* Buffalo, 1982, chapter 4.

Denominational Schooling in England and Wales

Sir Hermann Bondi

The school system of England and Wales is extraordinarily complex, arising as it does from compromises reached over many years. The modern system was enshrined in the Education Act of 1944, which, in spite of a number of amending acts, is still the basis of the whole system. The system is not centralized but is the responsibility of the numerous local education authorities. However, they all have to operate under the Act, which covers the whole country.

Basically, the Act distinguishes between county schools and voluntary schools. A county school is entirely the responsibility of the local education authority, though under the law one of their responsibilities is to provide religious instruction and to start the day at each school with a collective act of worship. This is not the topic of this note. Indeed the problems arising for freethinkers from these particular regulations are relatively modest. What is much more serious is the position of voluntary schools, which means essentially schools that exist in response to demand by religious communities. Provided that these satisfy certain general rules (such that they are open to inspection by Her Majesty's Inspectors of Schools), that they are staffed, and the staff paid in accordance with the general rules of the county and simi-

131

lar arrangements, these schools put a very small financial burden on the religious community but the faithful have a very considerable say in the running of them. The entire maintenance and running costs of such schools is borne by the local education authority who also pays a proportion of the capital costs arising from buildings, etc. Though this proportion was originally lower, it is now 85 percent, so the religious community has to find a mere 15 percent of the capital costs, thereafter everything else is paid for.

Until relatively recently, this system has not created any major problems in England and Wales. The Catholics are of course the main beneficiaries. Though there are many Church of England schools, these are in general not all that different from the county schools. There have also been for many years a few schools of other denominations, such as Methodist, Baptist, and Jewish. In as homogeneous a country as the British side at least of the United Kingdom was, the problems that have arisen have been minor. We have no anti-clerical party of any sort in the country and the parties of the Left and the Right generally tend to leave the denominational schooling issue completely untouched and have no particular views on it. Of course the same law operates in Northern Ireland where the divisions are very much deeper. The present tragic situation may indeed to a considerable extent be ascribed to the existence of separate schools. The majority in the province being Protestant and very conscious of their religion, the county schools are effectively Protestant schools. The limited amount of self-government that the province had until 1972 (and many features of which have effectively been continued) gave very full support to the schools of the Catholic minority operating under the same law as in England and Wales. This separate schooling under the guise of religion has effectively kept the communities apart, with the disastrous consequences we all know.

Moves toward integrated schooling are slowly growing but are fiercely resisted by both sides in the dispute. The great change that has come over England and Wales, which used to be so homogeneous a country, has arisen largely in consequence of immigration, notably Moslem immigration from the Indian subcontinent. The problem of the integration of ethnic minorities into the country as a whole is nowhere easy, but a serious problem we now face is that the Moslem communities ask to have their own special schools so that they can be single-sex schools and very much work on Islamic principles. Though these communities generally find it difficult to meet even the 15 percent requirement for capital equipment, gradually one, two, and more such schools will arise, thereby increasing the divisions in the country.

Though this is known to be a real problem, nobody seems prepared to grasp this nettle. But of course, if in so serious a matter nobody is prepared to tackle a difficult and controversial question, then this makes the law an excellent help to small sects, particularly if they are reasonably rich. Thus schools of various fundamentalist persuasions arise. There are one or two fundamentalist Jewish ones, and there are beginning to be fundamentalist Moslem schools, not to mention other openings for fundamentalist Christian sects.

Though there is wide agreement that these schools are not a good thing, it is exceedingly hard to imagine that a state authority can declare some religions as good and entitled to have their schools, and others as bad and not entitled to have them. So as long as we have this law there is no obvious way to resist the demands of smaller and smaller and, may I add, sometimes crazier and crazier communities for their schools.

The only safeguard we have at the moment concerns the general standard of schooling that children must receive. Her Majesty's Inspectorate of Schools is an able and very highly regarded body. Their function however is purely advisory. They have certainly criticized some such schools severely, not because they keep the children separate from others, not because they indoctrinate them in their particular vicious fundamentalism, but because the general education is bad. Naturally the communities resist, but where they have enough money there is of course no very great difficulty in improving the standard of general education to a level acceptable to the Inspectorate. It is one of the frustrating things for a humanist that one can see the evils of the present law, the evils of allowing denominational schooling and supporting it from public funds, and yet this is regarded as not a suitable question for political discussion because it would tear apart the established parties. Most politicians regard other questions as far more important and would not wish to see the damage arising from such a question ventilated. Others, including the present government, are very much in favor of schools that are based on communities even if they are exclusive. Thus we have a rather awkward situation for which no cure is obvious. Though, as I was saying, there is widespread agreement that these narrow fundamentalist sects are not to be encouraged, nobody seems to know how to stop encouraging them.

Surviving the Apocalypse

Gerald A. Larue

Forty-one years ago today, August 6th, at 8:15 a.m., a 6,000-pound payload was released from an American B-59 bomber named Enola Gay, flying at an altitude of 30,800 feet above the Japanese city of Hiroshima. The payload, an atomic bomb nicknamed "Little Boy," exploded at 1,980 feet above the city and the age of atomic warfare was introduced. The city was virtually annihilated.

Since that date in 1945, the world has entered the nuclear age. Nuclear power is utilized for peaceful purposes throughout the modern world, but as the disaster at Chernobyl has taught us, there can be heavy costs in human life—26 dead, 18,000 at risk, 100,000 resettled in the Soviet Union, with no way of knowing the results of fallout elsewhere. Nuclear weapons, far more sophisticated and deadly than "Little Boy" are stored, ready for use, in the Soviet Union, the United States, and among their allies. The potential is in hand for a nuclear holocaust that could destroy the world. The language that is often used to describe this devastating event is drawn from the Bible. We hear references to the Apocalypse, which is the title of the last book in the New Testament canon—a writing that is often titled "The Revelation to John" or just "Revelation." According to Rev. 16:16, the battle that will destroy the world is supposed to take place at *har Megiddo* or "the hill of Megiddo" or "Armageddon" in Israel. The site of ancient Megiddo has been partially excavated. It was the locale of several significant battles in biblical history.

The idea of a battle to end the world is popular among fundamentalist Christians, but it is not unique to our time. The history of the Christian Church is peppered with the accounts of those who, on the basis of events current with their epoch, interpreted biblical passages to prove that they were living in the last days, in the time of Armageddon. Indeed, these notions were popular throughout the Western world during the late nineteenth and early twentieth centuries. In each and every case, the prediction was wrong; the world continued on its course.

What fundamentalist Christians believe is, of course, their own business, but when apocalyptic or end-of-the-world thinking becomes popular and enters into the language of political leaders in powerful countries, it is time to take notice.

The American fundamentalist preacher Hal Lindsay has written a book titled *The Late Great Planet Earth*, which has become the best selling book of the past decade with sales exceeding 18,000,000 copies. Lindsay and another fundamentalist author, David Wilkerson, who wrote *Twenty-One Amazing Predictions*, use the Bible to interpret what they believe are the signs of end-time. Basing their predictions on passages found primarily in the books of Ezekiel, Daniel, and Revelation, they inform their readers that the Bible foretells an attack on Israel from the north by the Russians and from the east by the Arabs and the Chinese. The United States will come to Israel's defense. The invasion will be triggered by the Israel attempt to rebuild the ancient Jewish temple that the Romans destroyed some 1,900 years ago, on the site of the Dome of the Rock mosque, one of the three holiest shrines in Islam. The conflict will be a nuclear war which evangelistic voices hail as part of the divine plan for bringing human history to its termination.

Now we may scoff at the stupidity of this sort of biblicism. The notion that Jews and Christians who lived some 2,000 to 3,000 years ago were able to write about Russian, Chinese, or American powers that were not in existence in their time, is pure nonsense. However, if one believes that the Bible is the inspired word of God which gives clues to the end of the world, then what is nonsense to the skeptic is pure truth to the believer, who can argue that the Holy Spirit gave the inspired words one meaning in ancient time but the true meaning for our day.

What is most unsettling is that in the United States apocalyptic language and references to biblical prophecy have entered the highest echelons of government. For example, shortly before the bombing attack on the U.S. Marine headquarters in Beirut, Lebanon, President Reagan is reported to have told a pro-Israel lobbyist:

> You know, I turn back to your ancient prophets in the Old Testament and the signs foretelling Armageddon, and I find myself wondering if—if we're the generation that's going to see that come about. I don't know if you have noted any of these prophecies lately, but believe me, they certainly describe the times we're going through.

The president is not alone in his use of apocalyptic rhetoric. The idea appears in the language of other government officials.

But what about the general public? It is estimated that some 45 million Americans and Canadians listen regularly to radio and television evangelists who believe that the coming into being of the State of Israel was in accord with divine design as outlined in the Bible. They are told that Israelis will rebuild the temple, and that when nuclear war does occur, the good, believing Christians, including the likes of the Reverend Jerry Falwell, will be lifted up, together with the resurrected faithful dead, to meet Jesus, who will return to earth riding on clouds of glory—an event known as "The Rapture."

Interestingly enough, these Armageddon fundamentalists never seem to come under attack from the mainline churches, most of whom do not endorse this nonsensical interpretation of the Bible. There is good reason for the silence. Present-day end-of-the-world claims are based on the existence of the State of Israel. To attack the interpretation could be seen as a attack on Israel. This in turn could be seen as anti-Semitism and no one wants to be accused of that!

If the Bible is the source of apocalyptic ideas, what is apocalypticism and how did it happen to develop in ancient Israel?

The term "apocalyptic" means "revealed" and it refers to a kind of literature that blossomed in ancient Israel between the third century B.C.E. and the second century C.E. It predicted a violent, cataclysmic end to the present world and the coming-into-being of a new world. It developed during desperate, threatening times for orthodox Judaism and was a response to feelings of helplessness, despair, and even abandonment by their god. Permit me to explain this evolution.

During the sixth century B.C.E., Jews were taken into captivity in Babylon. They were freed and permitted to return to Palestine by Cyrus the Great. By the end of the fourth century B.C.E., Alexander the Great had overrun the world and the Jews were under Greek control. At Alexander's death, his empire was divided among his generals and Israel became a buffer state between Egypt, which was ruled by the Greek Ptolomies, and Syria, which was governed by the Greek Seleucids. Under the Seleucid king Antiochus IV, the Jews experienced tremendous attacks on their religion.

The Persians seem to have permitted the Jews to follow their own pattern of worship, but Alexander and his followers were convinced that the Greek way of life was the finest and best way to live and were determined to achieve unity among the conquered nations. They proposed that each nation would abandon traditional customs and conform to Greek patterns. When he was opposed by pious, orthodox Jews, Antiochus was furious. The author of I Maccabees described what happened in these words:

> Now on the 15th day of Chislev (December) in the one hundred and forty-fifth year (167 B.C.E.), they erected on the altar of burnt offering a desolating sacrilege (they burned pig's flesh). They also built altars in the surrounding cities in Judah, and burned incense at house portals in the streets. They ripped to pieces and burned Torah scrolls. And if the covenant book was found in anyone's possession, or if anyone obeyed the Torah, he was condemned to death by royal decree. . . . They killed women who had their children circumcised, along with their families and the circumciser, and then they hung the infants from the mothers' necks. (I Macc. 1:54–61)

Some Jews cooperated with the Greek decrees. They wore Greek clothing, ate Greek non-kosher food, and exercised in the nude in the gymnasium. Some went so far as to have the mark of circumcision removed (I Macc. 1:14–15).

It was during this period that biblical apocalypticism developed. The literature evolved from the impact of Persian or Aryan theology on Semitic or Jewish theology, engendered by the social and political situation.

Aryan theology was based on a revelation that was supposed to have been given to the prophet Zarathustra or Zoroaster by Theone, true, universal god, Ahura Mazda—the god of truth, of light, of goodness. According to Aryan theology, time was depicted as a segmented line extending from the beginning or creation to the end-of-world existence. There were different epochs beginning with the age of gold and succeeded by time periods of lesser value—silver, bronze, iron, and so on. Ultimately, time would run out and there would be a time of judgment for all souls. All would be judged and rewarded or punished according to the way in which they had behaved during their earthly lives.

Although Ahura Mazda was the only god, there was an anti-god power named Ahriman who represented the lie, darkness, and evil. Each individual chose whether to follow the way of truth or the way of the lie, the paths of light or the paths of darkness, to walk in the way of goodness with Ahura Mazda or in the way of evil with Ahriman. The individual's choice would determine that person's fate at the time of final judgment.

Through the impact of Persian culture, the Jews were introduced to cosmic dualism. Until that time their god, Yahweh, had been responsible for both good and evil. Now Yahweh, like Ahura Mazda, was separated from any taint of evil and he became, like the Aryan god, the embodiment of perfection—pure truth, pure goodness, pure righteousness. From their own mythology, the Jews chose a counterpart for Ahriman. Satan, who was also recognized as Belial, Beelzebub, or Lucifer, became the embodiment of anti-Yahweh power, competing for the souls of the Jews, and later of the Christians.

The fullest expression of apocalyptic thinking in the Jewish canon is in the book of Daniel, and in Christian scriptures the Book of Revelation. There were other apocalyptic writings from the same period that were not included in the canon and are now collected in the Pseudepigrapha. They include the books of Enoch, the Testament of the Twelve Patriarchs, the Assumption of Moses and the Apocalypse of Baruch.

The fundamental theological problem confronting the apocalyptic writer was theodicy—the justice of god. If Yahweh was the only deity and the paragon of virtue and goodness, and in control of the world, why did faithful Jews who followed his revealed ways suffer so terribly under Antiochus IV, while those who violated every revealed precept were free from persecution? The apocalyptic answer was that although evil appeared to be victorious, the victory was temporary. In the afterworld the scales of justice would be set right, the righteous would be rewarded; the evil would suffer through eternity.

The book of Daniel utilized the Zoroastrian time-line concept. Although the book was written in 167 B.C.E., it gave the appearance of being written during the Babylonian exile, which was described as the golden age. It then seemed to predict history by presenting what had already happened as though it was being foretold—thus the time of the Medes was the silver age, the Persian period the bronze, Alexander represented the iron age, and his successor the age of iron and mud that preceded the divine in-breaking. When the author attempted to forecast what would happen after 167 B.C.E. he was absolutely wrong. He told his readers that they were living in the last days, that suffering would soon cease and the divine kingdom of the faithful Jews would come into being. Utilizing the predictive mode, he wrote:

> In that time, the great (angelic) prince Michael who has the responsibility for your people will come forth. And there will be a period of trouble, the like of which has never before occurred, but then your people will be saved, every one whose name is recorded in the book. And many of those who are asleep in the earth's dust will awaken— some to everlasting life and some to everlasting contempt. (Dan. 12:1–2)

The chapter ends with a numerical code that signifies that end time would occur according to one passage within 3.5 years, and according to another within 7 years.

Like all apocalyptic writing, Daniel is characterized by secret codes. It must be remembered that this was underground literature, predicting the downfall of the existing government. The authors are never identified. They wrote in the name of some ancient worthy—Daniel or Enoch or Baruch—and who could prosecute the long dead? Numbers and beasts become symbols of monarchs and nations, which were clear to the initiated. History was distorted and given a deterministic interpretation: what had happened to the Jews was in accord with the divine will—Yahweh had revealed his intentions back in the Babylonian age to Daniel. If Daniel correctly foretold the succeeding nations, how could he err in revealing what would happen after Antiochus IV? No matter what humans did, nothing could change the plan—history was fixed, predetermined. The wise would keep the faith despite persecution and death, because they knew the end was at hand and they would be rewarded in the next life. In other words, apocalyptic writing was a message of hope in a time of despair and it encouraged stubborn belief and resistance.

Of course Daniel was wrong. Deliverance did not come through divine intervention but through the warlike activities of the Maccabees. For a brief time the Jews were free from external rule, but soon they became subjects of Rome.

When Christian teaching and writing began, apocalyptic thinking was part of current Jewish theology. Indeed the Essene community that existed on the shores of the Dead Sea during Jesus' lifetime were deeply immersed in apocalyptic theology. They believed the kingdom was at hand and that they were in the wilderness to prepare for it.

Jesus and his followers also believed they were living in end time. Over and over again New Testament writers tell us that Jesus spoke of the proximity of the divine kingdom. After Jesus' death, Christians taught that he had been miraculously resurrected, that he had ascended to heaven, and that he would soon return to establish the kingdom. So convinced were the Christians of Thessalonica that the event was at hand that some were neglecting social responsibilities to prepare for it. When the book of Revelation was written at the end of the first century C.E., the hope was still alive. John purported to reveal what must "soon take place" (1:1) and the book ends with the statement "He who testifies to these events says 'Truly, I am coming soon,' " to which the author added the cry "Amen! Come Lord Jesus!"

Well, Jesus was wrong. Paul was wrong. The New Testament writers were wrong. Through the ages all those who have believed have been wrong. Perhaps one may hazard a guess that present-day Bible interpreters, including President Ronald Reagan, are wrong. Doomsday will not come through a divine in-breaking. If it does come it will be the result of stupidity, greed, selfishness, indifference, anger, bitterness, and hatred.

We humanists do not look beyond our world for deliverance; we look to ourselves, who have created the problems, to solve them and redeem humankind. If there is to be an ideal world, then we who have the vision must bring that world into being and make that vision real.

Now, I would like to discuss three issues. The first is that biblical apocalyptic thinking is a destructive, devisive notion coming from a destructive, devisive book, the Bible.

Of course we can find high ethical concepts embedded in biblical writings, as we can in the teachings of most religions, but we can emphasize those noble ideals as reprsesenting biblical thought only by ignoring the general thrust of the Bible. There are passages that encourage one to seek justice, to love mercy, to treat one's neighbor as oneself, to accept the prodigal, to speak the truth, to promote understanding, to treat one another with dignity. These are excellent ethical ideals. But we do not need the Bible to tell us about noble human ideals. These sentiments have evolved over and over again in human societies; they are not uniquely biblical. What has happened is that in the Western world the Bible has been exalted until it has become, for some, the sole textbook for human values. The time has come when we need to admit that biblical thinking, which represents the viewpoints of small groups of people living in a corner of the Mediterranean world some 2,000 to 3,000 years ago, is largely unethical, destructive, and no longer adequate or relevant for use in this last fifth of the twentieth century.

Now let me support my argument. I find the Bible to be one of the most pessimistic and negative collections of writings in human history. It consists of religious failure fiction that records failures by the Jewish god Yahweh, who is angry and upset because he is not able to create a world that functions in accord with his wishes and intentions, and failure by a people who, despite their efforts, were unable to please their demanding deity. And even when Yahweh focused his energy on one minority group, they failed and angered him. In view of what we know of the psychology of failure, we can predict that the outcome of this kind of theology could only be continuous frustration, morbidity of spirit, and desperate, fruitless efforts at conformity that could only produce feelings of failure and helplessness. In our day, such feelings drive humans to seek solutions for their dejection in drugs, alcohol, sex, or whatever else might relieve tension. In those days, the clergy took advantage of every disaster to say "We told you so" and to urge greater conformity to their teachings.

To be more specific, we should note that the Bible opens with the creating of the world. In chapter 2 of the book of Genesis we are told of the forming of the first male, then of animals to be his companions, and finally of a female who is an extension of the male. The setting was idyllic. God and his creatures were together in harmony. Because the human couple disobeyed Yahweh, they were punished, dispossessed, expelled from their garden home.

In the external world they propagated. Their offspring attempted to reestablish the divine-human relationship by building a tower to link heaven, up there, with earth, down here. Yahweh was threatened and broke the spirit of cooperation and accord among humans by confusing their languages. We know that people who cannot talk together cannot work together, whether the impasse is interpersonal or international. Here, Yahweh is portrayed as a god of confusion—one who created the basis for misunderstandings among humans.

Another myth tells of divine creatures, the sons of god, coming to earth and impregnating earth women. For this act, humans were punished. Yahweh caused a flood that wiped out life on earth with the exception of the survivors of the ark, who were to replenish the life Yahweh destroyed in his fury.

From the descendants of the survivors, Yahweh chose one man and his wife: Abraham and Sarah. They were to be the founders of the chosen people of Yahweh. He provided Moses with the rules and regulations He demanded His people to obey, and He commissioned Aaron to develop priestly rites for sacrifices and offerings to please Him and keep Him satisfied. But the Jews failed their god. In his anger, Yahweh sent Assyrians to annihilate the ten northern tribes and the kingdom of Israel; he sent the Babylonians to massacre Jews in Judah and to enslave a remnant as captives in Babylon. After the exile, the remnant Jews were subject to Persian and Greek overlords. The conditions under Antiochus IV were so harsh that the Jews suffered a failure of nerve and it was then that apocalyptic notions became part of their religion.

The apocalyptic idea became part of developing Christian thought. Christian fiction explained it this way: Because Yahweh found it impossible to be reconciled to his creatures, he sent his own son Jesus into the world of humans. The divine anger could only be appeased by an offering of human flesh and blood, hence this loving father-god had his own son killed because human sinners had failed to live up to divine imperatives. According to this story, this frightening angry god could think of no other way to make his people acceptable except through violence, suffering and the death by torture of his own son.

But even this salvation is limited. One can be saved only if Christian atonement concepts are accepted, only if one will close eyes to the psychosocial sickness of these teachings and acknowledge the validity of the toxic prescription. Even among Christians there are ongoing disputes and divisions concerning which group is truly acceptable to this disturbed deity. As for the rest of us, we go to hell for eternity. Revelation reads:

> And I saw the dead, the great and the small, standing before the throne, and the books were opened. . . . And the dead were judged by what was written in the books, by what they had done . . . and if anyone's name was not found written in the book of life, he was tossed into the lake of fire. (Rev. 20:12–15)

Christians must know their imperfections. They cannot measure up to Jesus' edict "Be perfect, just as your heavenly father is perfect" (Matt. 5:48). No one has ever satisfied Yahweh. Despite the theology that says that Jesus took on himself their imperfections and died in their stead, Christians can only continue to be insecure. The gloomy smoke of hell fire hangs over them just as the shadow of mushroom clouds hangs over the entire world.

Evangelicals say they do not fear nuclear war, because this may be God's way of ending the whole human drama. They will be part of the eternal kingdom. There can be no ecological concern here, any more than there was in Yahweh when he sent the flood. Why should they worry about toxic pollution or the extinction of life forms with the destruction of rain forests. Why be concerned about the future of humankind? The future is predetermined. The end is at hand. Be concerned only about your status when the final judgment comes.

Biblical religion and biblical apocalypticism portray an angry, destructive, abusive father figure in God. He requires absolute, blind obedience from those who would be among his chosen ones. In that very demand are the elements of irresponsibility for the well-being of humans. The Kingdom of Armageddon Christians is not of this world and the sooner it comes, the better. I find it frightening when I think of the many who accept this fiction as fact, uncritically, unquestioningly. What is most unnerving is to know that a world leader, a man with the power to initiate an atomic war, accepts this kind of theology.

My second point is related to what I am calling "the uncertainty principle." Traditional religions offer certainty: this is who you are, this is how you came into being, this is the meaning of our existence, this is the purpose of your life. They provide a neat package of preformed answers.

For the rest of us, when through scientific and technological research we move into the far reaches of the universe, or into the minute dimensions of the atom, we become aware that we are truly happenstance creatures. Our studies in the generational processes reveal that whether one is male or female depends upon which sperm, of millions ejaculated in a single act of intercourse, first reaches and penetrates the ovum plus the genetic codes brought to the union by the sperm and ovum. Had another sperm penetrated the ovum, a different person would have resulted. We begin our existence as happenstance creatures.

Unless we accept the notion that there is some ultimate purpose supporting the universe, all that is and all that we are as individuals or as humans is the result of the happenstance clash of atoms. Our birth, our life setting, and so on are happenstance. This can be hard to accept, because in effect it says "You are important because you happen to exist."

This idea sets our ethics on a survival course. What must I do to survive? so that you can survive? so that the families in Ethiopia or Afghanistan or India can survive? The ethics focuses on the preservation of this life form, which has evolved out of the eons of time. How does this kind of thinking affect our ethical perspectives? We might state that our highest ethics have developed out of the long human search for meaning, for identity, for survival, even as we wrestle with our awareness of the uncertainty principle. And we are able to admit: this is what we think we know now in the light of the evidence in hand. Tomorrow, new discoveries, new insights may cause us to rethink and reevaluate what we believe today. We know that new Galileos, new Einsteins, new Gandhis are constantly being born.

There is dynamic energy in the uncertainty approach because we are always in process, always evolving, always developing, always becoming. Our significance as individuals is based on our acceptance of the happenstance dimension of our existence. Our awareness of the long, long eons of time that have passed before the unique individual that is each one of us evolved—each one absolutely unique, never to be duplicated, with absolutely unique experiences and unique interpretation of those experiences, can prompt each of us to state "I do not know the origins of all that is or even of my own personal existence, but I know that I am here, I have a terminus and my life will end. Therefore it is important that I make decisions about what life style, what life-qualities will bring to my existence the greatest exuberance, the highest joys, the deepest meaning, the most satisfaction." From the great thinkers of the past and present, from philosophers and psychologists, artists, theologians, skeptics, scientists, from builders and workers, dreamers and plodders I have been provided with insights and guidelines that will enrich my existence and give my life meaning—not meaning based on religious fiction about a god or gods, nor on theories about rewards and punishments in the afterlife, or about what happens if I have a disaffected karma or if I fail to follow certain rules and regulations or responses, but meaning of life that brings to me and to others the most rewarding, the most uplifting, and the most satisfying of human experiences.

I express concern for my fellow creatures not only because I have been raised in a social environment, or because I have learned through insights transmitted from the past that wise men have always recognized our social nature, but also because when we study the ways of wild creatures that have not been exposed to our social conditioning, we discover that they, too, are social creatures. Somehow, in ways we do not yet understand they communicate with one another and appear to have some sort of mutuality of understanding. Until recently, humans have believed that they were the only rational creatures. Now we are becoming aware that social patterns have evolved among other earth creatures and have been transmitted through what we in our ignorance call "instinct." This suggests that the evolutionists' claim that we are kin to other creatures has wide ramifications. My concern for humans and for other life forms appears to be basic to my nature. I need others to express my humanity and my oneness with the world. My communal concerns are related to my basic communal nature. Inasmuch as we have developed the technological skills for destroying life, our survival ethics might well embrace a deep concern for all life forms.

Perhaps because we have placed so much emphasis on our rationality, and our rationality combined with our technological and scientific enterprise has brought us face to face with potential total destruction, we may, in frustration, end up distrusting both the scientific and the rational processes. We then become endangered because we might just begin to agree with the fundamentalists and with certain biologists who argue that humans cannot be trusted to be rational or to use science and technology humanely, and that therefore we need strong controls. The fundamentalists would argue that Christian ethics, undergirded by apocalytpic theology, provide the very curbs necessary.

Many feel a deep need for sure answers and controls. But fixed answers and controls limit growth, stifle experimentation, lock us into given patterns, and deny the questing spirit by reducing life to a regimen. Boundaries are useful for definitions, but fixed boundaries negate the visions that engender change and refuse space for the creative spirit to soar beyond the given.

As humanists we are committed to open inquiry, to free inquiry. We cannot accept a religion that tells us the future is fixed and predetermined. We recognize that Ashley Montague was on target when he pointed out that "religion gives us certainty without proof; science gives us proof without certainty." The way of ethical humanism is the latter; the way of apocalypticism is the former.

My final point deals with the passivity and the message of helplessness that is at the core of apocalypticism. It tells us that we cannot overcome the forces of darkness that would diminish our humanhood, that work to destroy our dreams and our hopes for humankind. It tells us that we can only bow before the overwhelming strength of war-minded governments, of profit-centered corporations, of selfish indifference to human well-being and dismissal of the significance of starvation and suffering, persecution and enslavement, denial of rights and destruction of spirit. These are patterns associated with the final destruction of the world before God breaks in and delivers the faithful.

We do not believe we are helpless. Powers can be challenged. Changes can be effected. We have the witness of history to sustain our faith. It is because humans have challenged the authority of civil and religious rulers that democracy has emerged; women have been emancipated; child labor laws have been enacted; private ownership has expanded; and that the benefits of adequate food, clothing, shelter, and loving care have touched more than ever before in history. And we acknowledge that the task is still before us. We are not caught up in the apocalyptic dream of divine deliverance for the select few—a doctrine that separates humans and sets them one against the other; a belief that anticipates with broad acceptance the potential horrors of a nuclear war. We cannot accept the fundamentalist denial of the scientific method, or the use of logic and the rational process as a means to progress. We deny that all wisdom has been given in the past. We admit that our social, scientific, and technological growth needs to be controlled by humanitarian concerns and by ethical commitment that seeks to develop the highest and the best in each human. Nor can we accept the apocalyptic vision of the end of the world. The future is in process and we, the present, are part of that process, developing the emerging future, conditioning, helping that which is to come to be imbued with ethical and moral concerns. I will close with the words of Felix Adler. He wrote:

> We live in order to finish an, as yet, unfinished universe, unfinished so far as the human, that is, the highest part of it, is concerned. We live in order to develop the superior qualities of the human which are, as yet, for the most part latent.
>
> The test of genuine moral culture is to be found in the attention we pay to the oft-neglected details of conduct; in the extent to which we have formed the habit of asking: What is it right to do in those little things which yet are not little?
>
> The thought of the brevity of life is the prod that spurs us on to the achievement of our task: it is like the blast

of a bugle from the walls of a fortress that warns us to make haste lest the gates be closed against us.

We are to go out as teachers among the people, discarding the limitations imposed by the theologies of the past, and holding up the moral ideal, pure and simple, as the human ideal, as the ideal for all, embracing all, binding on all—the ideal of a perfect society, of a society in which no men or women or class be mere hewers of wood and drawers of water for others; in which no man or woman, or class of men or class of women shall be used as tools for the lusts of others; or for the ambitions of others, or for the greed of others; in which every human life, the life of every man and woman and child, shall be esteemed a sacred utterance of the Infinite.

Yes to Life

Sir Hermann Bondi

We humanists are, almost everywhere, a minority, a minority in our thinking, a minority in our attitudes. Various criticisms are thrown at us. And what I would like to do today is to give you a little more ammunition to throw back when such criticisms against our views are voiced.

First, there is the suggestion that we have too optimistic, too rosy a view of the nature of human beings. I don't think that is in the least correct. We take human beings as they are. Humanism means that. It means that we accept ourselves, with our limitations, with our handicaps, with our advantages. And we try to make the best of this, not because we believe that we are perfect, but because we profoundly believe we are what we are and there is nothing better available. It is no use asking for something superior if something superior does not exist, or at the least is not accessible to us. We have got to make do with ourselves as we are. This rather simple statement is important, because quite a number of things follow from it. It does not mean that we think every one of our features are perfect. That, of course, would be absurd—even if we just look at it from an evolutionary point of view. A former colleague of mine was very much interested in mammals in general, and those of Antarctica in particular. And after some quite involved counts of a particular kind of seal, he said that this must be the most abundant, the most numerous of all large mammals, because there are 40 to 50 million of them. "Oh no," I said, "I know of a large mammal that is much more abundant in numbers. Ourselves." We are not fully adjusted to the enormous number of us who, with unbelievable success, people the globe. It is a marvelous success for our species that we can live in such a multitude. But that we are not perfectly adapted to our own numbers should not surprised us. And this leads to certain dangerous characteristics to which others have already referred. But if we look at our own nature, we say "yes" to it. We take a positive attitude. The first characteristic I want to discuss here is our sexuality.

So many religions regard our sexuality as either a bad feature—one barely to be tolerated—or if tolerated, then only in a very highly defined and prescribed manner. But it is an enormously important human characteristic, which finds many different kinds of expression. To say that we know that only one approach to sexuality is right is a degree of intolerance we do not arrogate to ourselves, as so many of our religious friends are ready to do. We admire sexuality because it brings people together. We admire it because it brings happiness. Of course we are worried if it is used to hurt people. Anything that affects us strongly can cause injury as well as happiness. But we do believe we take ourselves as we are, and not according to some abstract model that somebody has devised of what we *ought* to be like. It is this desire of putting us into a mould that I find so singularly repulsive in so many attempts at creating a prescriptive view of the world, whether religious or nonreligious. Such views oppose humanism by not recognizing our variety. It is our task as humanists to be very pleased with, to enjoy the variety of human beings in their many different ways. Our species has done so well because we are not clones of each other.

It is our individuality that we want to admire and foster, not some pre-defined mould or form. Because we say "yes to life," we see no merit in mortifying the flesh, in bleeding in public. We recognize that some people have different wishes and desires than others. We like our human variety. The adulation of virginity, present in so many Christian churches, and the separation of women, so strong in Islam, are not part of our value system. If somebody feels like remaining a virgin—good luck. That is their way of living, which we regard as neither superior nor inferior, but as their free choice. But to hold this out as a model for everybody, something to be admired, is absurd and, as my more theological friends tell me, it may be due to nothing more than a mistranslation from the Hebrew.

Similarly, we admire our social instincts. If we did not want to be with each other, we would find life very hard. And as the congress president has reminded us, we might find death even harder. It is because we live in each other and through each other, through influencing each other and communicating with each other, that human existence gains its value. And some of this value lives in others after we die. This mutual dependence is something very important to us. What has allowed us to engage in it is of course our wonderful invention of speech. And through it we can enjoy a complex variety of relationships, a variety that is quite astonishing and central to our positive attitude toward humanity.

It is implicit in this joy in variety that we do not like to divide or to exclude. I do not like to be told that a particular hotel or club is very exclusive. I like to know who they exclude. And I do not believe that it is our humanist wish to separate people, to divide them by one means or another. I think that perhaps our most powerful charge, our most powerful accusation against religions, is that they divide people from each other. It is very hard for anybody to deny that there are different religions in the world, that people in each may be very sincere, very intelligent, very determined, even very good. But they will tend to think that they alone are right, and that others are wrong; that they are separate from others, and so they divide people. In the United Kingdom we see this close at hand through our unfortunate experiences in Northern Ireland. As I like to say, if you try to divide children by the length of their eyebrows, people will think you are insane and have you treated. If you want to divide them by the color of their skin, you are rightly put in jail. But if you want to divide them by their religion, somehow everybody applauds. This seems to me stark, staring mad. We cannot tolerate this. And if I may go on for a moment about Northern Ireland, the Protestant majority was dominant for many years. If one asked them then what were they doing for the Catholic minority, they would proudly say they were living up to the letter of the law by generously supporting their schools. This effort divided the two communities with the tragic results that we have seen now for many decades. The divisiveness that is so strong between two religions as close to each other as two brands of Christianity, goes much further, is even worse, where the religions are further from each other, as we can see in so many parts of the world. Because we say "yes to life" we detest divisions. We want to abolish divisions, or at the very least moderate and ameliorate them as fast as we can. With our joy in human variety, racism and sexism are just not feasible with us. This does not mean that we are perfect. It only means that such attitudes are incompatible with our basic principles.

Now another very important human characteristic that we must accept is that we are often wrong. To be cock-sure is not given to us. We are not like that. And most of us, most of the time, realize that possibility. But our religious friends are not so modest. To put it a trace unkindly, they believe that they have a private telephone line to the office of the Almighty. I think this is the crucial division; that they have a degree of certainty that we would never aspire to, that we regard as profoundly inhuman. Let me become a trifle more complicated: When I am asked whether I am an atheist—I say that I do not regard this as a meaningful question—I can only say "no" to something that is defined, not to something that is a wholly nebulous concept. If somebody tells me God is life, I am not going to deny life. If somebody tells me God is nature, I am no going to deny nature. Where my division with religious people lies is not over the concept of God, undefined as it is. It is over revelation. I declare myself a total anti-revelationist. It is because our religious friends, so many of them, not necessarily of every persuasion but of most, believe they have direct access to *sure* knowledge, that they are capable of such monstrous behavior, and such cruelties as cover the pages of history in religious fighting. Whenever one is too sure, whenever one has a vision—a very clear and definite, maybe even beautiful vision—of man's place, whether as a Marxist or as a Catholic, or a Muslim or an Orthodox Jew, whenever you have a perfect vision, then you are prepared to sacrifice yourself, for sure. But they are willing to sacrifice everybody else too. It is not that these people are necessarily selfish; much worse, they are dangerous. It is the dangers of certainty, of this unnatural and inhuman certainty, that is so profoundly worrying. Of course we have all got to make decisions; we have all got to make choices. Worse than that, the pressures of life mean that every one of us has to make decisions on insufficient evidence. That is the nature of the situation. And that is what life, to which we so emphatically say yes, is all about. But when we make such decisions, on evidence that is inevitably incomplete, we have got to tell ourselves what sacrifices we are asking other people to make because we have made a choice. All along the way we have to make choices. All along the way we are uncertain. That is what being human is about. And we have to recognize this and allow for it. We should be aware that not all human beings have the same view. Some feel just too damn certain. And one should always be suspicious of that.

With our joy in the variety of human beings, humanists are by nature tolerant. But we are certainly intolerant of intolerance. Intolerance exercised for religious, or possibly political reasons, is something we are undoubtedly against. I sometimes think maybe the only thing of which we humanists are wholly intolerant, is intolerance. I am not quite sure that that is entirely true, and it is a difficutl subject. When we see the attitude of the more reactionary Muslims to women, are we tolerant of that? I am not talking of their being in any way violent or brutal in this, but are we tolerant of them indoctrinating young women with these views that condemn them to a second-rate status? I am putting this question on the table. Does our tolerance extend to such teaching? I am a little doubtful. Certainly our fury is above all reserved for intolerance, but we should be rather careful about the limits we set to our own tolerance.

Our president has reminded us how much we should admire nature, of which we are a part. Yet I find it very difficult to be regretful of the eradication of smallpox, which is part of nature. And so it is again a human characteristic that there are very few things that we can carry through to their brutal, logical conclusion. We are a moderate, even illogical lot. Let us recognize this, and let us be pleased about it. It makes life fun. If it were all too logical, it could be an awful bore.

In our attitudes, then, we certainly want to be positive, we want to accept our nature. We want to recognize that we are creatures, not just of genetics, important as this is, but of culture. Certain cultural traditions and attitudes are those we want to foster. Others we are not so keen on. Our very admiration for the human ability to take responsibility means that by necessity we are democrats. We cannot imagine a situation in which, rightfully, a small group should arrogate themselves responsibility for others without asking them, individually, to take their own responsibility themselves. And it is the stress of individual responsibility that is the hallmark of democracy. Do not think it lies just in voting. Lobbying and pressure groups are as much part of a democracy as a parliament is. But it is individual responsibility that is so vital. Certainly we can only recognize as legitimate a government that is responsible to its people. Any other I certainly view as utterly irresponsible. It would be a misreading of the human character to think that a responsible democratic government is necessarily always a good government. It need not even be a very peaceable government. Do not let us fool ourselves. We have strong aggressive instincts, and we can be quite democratic yet aggressive. Nonetheless, there is no way of arrogating responsibility, of making a specialty of taking responsibility. It belongs to all of us, because we are all human beings, because we all say "yes to life."

Ethics in a Global Perspective

Johan Galtung

1. DEVELOPMENT THEORY IN CRISIS

Development theory is a *holistic* approach to human society, in principle, and *dynamic,* as the word indicates. It shares holism with such approaches as peace studies, future studies, and women's studies, all of them relatively recent, and all of them also reactions against the fragmentation of the study of the human condition into all kinds of specialties.

However, the practice has become sadly different. Instead of holism there has been a focus on economic aspects of the *social* space of human existence; instead of dynamism in an endogenous sense there has been a focus on the capacity to emulate certain societies held to be "developed," according to the now classical less developed countries (LDC), more developed countries (MDC), and Washington, D.C., model. This type of approach, which has shown a remarkable ability to survive the presumably mortal attacks directed against it, has left out *nature* space, the setting for ecological development, or at least balance, on which the human condition is absolutely predicated; it has left out the (inner) *human* space of mental/ spiritual development; it has left out other aspects of the social space although there is now—largely thanks to "Reaganism"— a renewed interest in political development and theory of democracy, and, it has left out the whole *world* space of regions and countries in conflict and cooperation. The latter has led to absurdities in the theory: if all countries have as a goal trade surplus and positive balances in general, then there is an obvious problem somewhere. In general, nobody seems to care whether societies held to be "developed" are mutually compatible in a global system.

So, we are left with a "theory" of development so miserable that it was incapable of foreseeing the ecological imbalances, incapable of taking into account the "civilization" diseases to the human *body* (cardiovascular diseases and tumors), mind (mental disorders), and *spirit* (a general sense of meaninglessness), incapable of handling problems of gross social maldevelopment (e.g., bureaucratization, militarization, and other forms of top-heaviness; lack of participation in general; flagrant inequalities). The point here is not that the practice was unable to solve these problems; the point is rather that the problems were not accommodated within the theory, not foreseen by that crisis-ridden body of thought.

The following, then, are some thoughts about alternative theories or theory, giving an approach that is totally different, where suddenly India, for instance, stands out as much more developed in basic ways than Norway, in spite of the latter being much richer per capita in economic terms (but not in terms of a concept of richness to be developed below).

2. FOUR SPACES AND THE ASSUMPTION OF ISOMORPHISM

We keep the assumption of development theory as holistic, and interpret this term so as to cover four spaces: nature, human, social, and world spaces. We also keep the assumption of development theory as dynamic, and interpret this as meaning changes toward some kind of "good" society, but on its own premises, not assuming any universal definition of 'good' except, perhaps, at a high level of generality and abstraction. In other words, holism, dynamism, and ameliorism are the benchmarks of development theory.

Looking at the four spaces there is no scarcity of approaches. For *nature* space there is the entire school of ecological balance. For the *human* body there is the medical tradition focusing on somatic health, and on mental health; and then the whole religious tradition focusing on spiritual health or salvation. For *social* space there are all the programs for social betterment built into social structure, culture, and ideology. And for *world* space there are the programs built into large "chunks" of humankind, the social cosmologies of civilizations. But there is no program for world society as such, except as projections from countries (e.g., federations, like the United States and the Soviet Union, seeing an extension of themselves to "United States of the World" and "World Soviet Socialist Republics" as desirable and attainable goals for the whole world). The world space—being the basic arena where peace is to be achieved—has yet to be mapped with a theory that is *sui generis,* at the world space level, and not some kind of reductionism to social, human, and/or nature levels (which, of course, would be included in theories of peace, only that the world level will have to play a major role).

Imagine that we now, as a point of departure, assume that there must be some basic similarity in the logic of balance in the four spaces, and that balance is at least a major component for *self-generated reproduction;* the system continues on its own engine so to speak. We are then left with two possibilities: using the theory of balance based on *one* of the spaces, or develop a totally new theory, a general systems theory, to cover *all* of them as "systems." Both approaches are meaningful, but in the present paper I shall stick to the former, perhaps trying to enrich it a little with concepts from the latter. And that raises the second basic question: from which space to learn?

I think there are three good reasons to try to learn from the *nature* space:

(1) Nature has been around much longer than we have. As a whole it has changed and differentiated, evolved what is usually referred to as higher forms—we humans arrogating to ourselves the title as the highest. Consequently, there must be some inherent "wisdom of nature," whatever its roots, something from which we can learn.

(2) Nature space is basic, all the others depend on it; whereas nature can very well survive without human beings around, without their social and global spaces. We depend on nature, not nature on us: we even destroy nature as evidenced by the ecological crisis today, and more so than nature has been destroying us (through natural calamities of various kinds). While the whole cosmic eco-chain has cosmo-, atmo-, hydro-, litho- and biosphere as its basis, the homosphere is a highly expendable tail.

(3) Perhaps our insight into nature is better than our insight into ourselves. This may be due to several reasons, of which two stand out. There is a distance between ourselves and the rest of nature that perhaps facilitates objectivity, insight, knowledge, whatever one might call it. Of course, *a priori* we might assume even more insight into the other three spaces since we are in them, of them, and by them. But precisely for that reason it may be more difficult to achieve the distance necessary to arrive at some fruitful general conceptualizations. We are too close to see our-

selves, there is too much at stake in our subjective values and interests. And then: could it not also be that natural scientists are simply, *grosso modo,* better at that game, at doing science, I mean?

However, let me add that when for these three reasons nature space is used in this context as the model for the other three, it is only seen as *one* possible approach, as something to be tested for its heuristic value.

In doing so, the point of departure is, of course, the general theory of ecological balance in *nature space.* By that we would now mean a nature space that includes not only abiota (in other words, the atmo-, hydro-, and lithosphere), but also biota (microorganisms, plants, animals). For the present purpose it is sufficient to state what seems to be a basic insight in ecological balance as follows: it is based on *diversity* and *symbiosis.* There is a certain plausibility to this: if a given part of nature space has sufficient diversity in abiota and biota (including access to the energy from the cosmosphere, solar energy in particular), and its diversity is made use of by the system for symbiosis so that the parts relate to each other, interact with each other, generate new abiota and biota in repeated or changing (or both) exchange cycles, then after some time a form of reliable balance should be the result.

This is plausible, also because it is so easily seen how a system in nature space might collapse: through lack of diversity (the abiota/biota needed are simply not available any longer), or through malfunctioning of the symbiotic mechanism. The former is seen in monocultural agriculture, which has to be maintained artificially by supplying diversity through manures and pesticides. And the second is seen in the nuclear winter, where the basic assumption in the scenario is that due to clouding of the atmosphere the interaction with cosmosphere is reduced so that a major form of symbiosis in nature space no longer functions, photosynthesis.

We shall refer to the joint functioning of diversity and symbiosis as "system maturity," and the general line of thought, for all four spaces, will be as indicated in Table 1.

The reader will find on the left the four spaces and along the top, nine headings where the first two are simply the spaces and subspaces. There are the obvious subdivisions of nature space. Then comes the human body, *soma,* that can be seen as a part of the *human space,* but certainly also as a part of the biosphere. The choice made here is in favor of the former. In that connection it should also be pointed out that a distinction has been made between *mind* and *soul:* the former is seen as the seat of emotions and cognitions, the latter as the seat of reflections on many things, among them emotions and cognitions of oneself and of others—in other words, of self-reflection. In principle, this would also include reflections on one's own capacity for reflection; in other words, philosophy. And so on, *ad infinitum.* It is this complexity that constitutes the *personality,* without necessarily having any clear view of where the line should be drawn between the mind and the soul, of whether the personality does also include aspects of the body in a purely somatic sense.

In *social space* a distinction has been made between the micro, meso, and macro levels. The former is the small group surrounding any individual, usually based on kinship and/or friendship, in other words, primary relations; the second would be the local level of social organization in a territorial sense and secondary associations usually based on values and/or interests in a social sense. The latter would be the national level, or tertiary relations (based on primary and secondary relations).

Finally, there is the *world space,* of interacting social spaces of all kinds. Much attention is paid these days to macro

Table 1
DEVELOPMENT GOALS: A SYSTEMIC APPROACH

(1) SPACE	(2) SUB-SPACE	(3) CODE	(4) SYSTEM MAINTE-NANCE (by definition)	(5) SYSTEM MATURITY (diversity and symbiosis)	(6) REPRO-DUCTION (using maturity)	(7) RESILIENCE (to violence)	(8) RESILIENCE (to exploitation)	(9) MAINTE-NANCE GOAL
NATURE	cosmosphere; atmo; hydro; litho; biosphere	genetic code	bio-*needs*	several bio-topes and exchange cycles	renewal	injury to needs	injury to renewal capacity	*eco-balance*
HUMAN	body - soma mind - psyche soul - spirit	genetic code personality	bio-*needs* other human *needs*	several homo-topes and exchange cycles	reproduction recovery	injury to needs	injury to reproduction recovery capacity	*health*
SOCIAL	micro - primary meso - local, secondary macro - national tertiary	structure culture ideology	social *interests*	several socio-topes and exchange cycles	reconstruction	injury to interests	injury to reconstruction capacity	*development*
WORLD	regional global	cosmology global/human cosmology	regional *interests* global *interests*	different systems in active and peaceful coexistence	reconstruction	injury to interests	injury to reconstruction capacity	*peace*

social spaces, in the sense of nation-states, and to the world as the system of nation-states. Nobody will deny the importance of this, but it leaves out all international, transnational and subnational actors that also may be operating in the world space. So I prefer to keep the concept more open. However, regardless of what kind of actors one can find in this space, a distinction between the global system encompassing all actors of that kind and a regional system composed of only a subsystem makes sense, particularly, for nation-states.

THE CODE OF SYSTEMS

Looking at the second column, what one finds is a very conventional hierarchy of increasing complexity, starting with cosmic energy and solar rays, and ending with world systems. It is a hierarchy of Chinese boxes, open one and inside you find the next level; open that one and you find the next one, and so on. But each space is steered by its own logic; each space has what is in the third column referred to as a *code,* which can also be referred to as a *program.* The programs are rules of transformation, defining processes of that space as goal-seeking entities, with complex feedback relations.

Thus, each organism in the *nature space,* in the biosphere, is the carrier of a genetic code that can be transmitted through acts of reproduction. The genetic code gives us the upper and lower limits of that entity, in terms of differentiation, complexity, etc. This also goes for the somatic aspect of human beings. But in addition human beings have personalities which we define as the code for the nonsomatic aspect. These are the propensities of mind and soul, the characteristics that make it easy for us to recognize a person from one day to the next since the personality remains more or less the same even if some manifestations change, depending on the weather, what happened early in the morning, the food eaten late at night and what not. A dramatic aspect of the spiritual capacity of a human being is the capacity to reflect on one's own personality, and not only reflect on it but possibly even change it, or change that of others, in any kind of "brainwashing," perceived as voluntary or involuntary by that person. Which of course makes one ask whether it is given to human beings, through spiritual means, also to change their own genetic code as some yoga practices possibly indicate.

Then there is the *social space*. The code is here seen as being built into the structure and the culture in an implicit form, and into the ideology in an explicit form—"explicit" meaning "spelled out."

In *world space* this becomes more complex since we are dealing with larger systems, bringing together many entities from social space. At this level it makes sense to talk about "deep structure" and "deep culture," meaning by that structural and cultural elements that seemingly different societies or systems in a *region* have in common. One might see them as the expression of a "deep ideology," and that is what is here referred to as (social) *cosmology*—the "personality of a civilization," to put it that way. And that of course raises the question whether there is such a thing as a code for a true world space, encompassing everything, a deep human ideology beyond the genetic code that humans have in common.

THE MAINTENANCE OF SYSTEMS

Let us now go on to the next column of "system maintenance." The two key concepts in this column are "needs" and "interests." We shall define them as the *conditio sine qua non* for system maintenance. If the needs of an organism are not satisfied then that organism disintegrates. This also applies to human beings, as biological organisms. And our needs can probably best be understood by studying the structure and function of the human being as a biological organism (in other words, anatomy and physiology), paying particular attention to the orifices of the body that should function (air, water, and food should be let in, excrement out; sensory impressions should be let in, mental reactions be permitted to come out; and so on. There is need for rest, there is need for activity. The list can be made long. Look at the list, put minuses in front of one or more of the items and you have a list of pain techniques, well-known to those who inflict punishment, even torture in all the social subspaces, from time immemorial, including parents.

Maybe it can be argued that these bioneeds for human beings fall into two categories: simple *survival,* which at the individual level means not succumbing to violence—direct or structural—and at the collective level, in addition to that, it also means procreation, that the human race will continue. And then, on the other hand, there is the need for something more than that, let us simply call it human *well-being,* the basic constituent in the World Health Organization definition of health.

It is readily seen how dependent all of this is on nature. Nature is the space in which we rest and are active. Nature supplies most of the absolutely indispensable inputs and receives (and transforms) some of our outputs. For nature to be able to accommodate, as a host, human beings, it has to be strong, particularly if human beings act like parasites. And since humans are biological organisms with personalities, they have other needs than bioneeds that may be incompatible with the stability of the nature space in which they are embedded, leading to exploitation of nature, to expansionism, etc.

How, then, does one approach the problem of nonbiological human needs? I have tried to classify them in two groups: *identity* needs and *freedom* needs. They are dialectically related. Identity needs demand some fixed point, some nucleus around which the individual can build and extend unions over and above himself as a biological organism, and the freedom needs are the needs for space, for somatic, psychological and spiritual movement, in search of union or away from union. Maybe the freedom needs also include the needs to be able to *escape from oneself,* in other words, to change, from time to time, the programs or codes embedded in one's personality?

Let me from these remarks proceed to the complex subject of *interests,* in social space and global space. What would be the interest of a social system or a system of social systems, whether the latter is regional or global? How, for instance, could one today conceive of "national interests," to take as an example a major type of social entry? Cutting through a long debate, could one not simply say that *a social system has but one legitimate interest: that of satisfying the basic needs, biological and nonbiological, of its members?* And then one can discuss who the members are, are they only human beings, or could they also include other biological organisms? In that case, would it include all animals or only some of them? I do not claim to have an answer: I only think that these questions should never be eliminated from the agenda of a good society.

I would then say that the same applies to more complex groupings, systems, or social systems at any level of complexity, filling ultimately the world space. The world interest is to satisfy the interests of *its* members, the interests of its members are to satisfy the needs of *its* members. But since the latter eventually depend on nature space, there is a limit to the extent to which one can get around satisfying the bioneeds of all organisms. And since the needs of organisms also depend on abiota, there is a limit to the extent to which one can destroy them. So, ultimately, we depend on ecological balance in a superspace comprising all four spaces.

THE MAJORITY OF SYSTEMS

And that leads us to the fifth column: "system maturity." This is where the bald assumption enters: System maturity is by definition based on the level of diversity combined with the level of symbiosis (between the components that constitute the diversity). The assumption, then, is that the higher the level of system maturity, the more resilient is the system, the more able to reproduce both in the sense of maintaining itself and creating new generations, or withstanding various types of injuries, even of setting goals for itself, realistically, within the conditions of system maturity.

In all spaces this calls for several types and symbioses. Let us refer to these types as *biotopes* in nature space, *homotopes* in human space, and *sociotopes* in the social and global spaces. Let us further assume a logic of Chinese boxes: the global space is an extremely rich sociotope, but so far in interaction with no other sociotope. Inside that sociotope there are social systems that may be exemplars of the same or different sociotopes, meaning social systems or societies, within those sociotopes there may again be, at lower levels of complexity, the same or different sociotopes, until one comes down to homotopes, human beings that may or may not be of the same or different types and may or may not have different homotopes or inclinations, propensities that are more or less developed.

Thus, on the one hand one could imagine a world space consisting of a number of societies exactly of the same type, based on exactly the same (and low) numbers of components, populated by human beings of a very uniform kind, who inside themselves have cultivated exactly the same (and in low numbers) inclinations. Then, on the other hand, there would be a world with very different societies that inside themselves would have very diverse components, all of this in very complex cycles of interaction; populated by very diverse human beings who inside themselves would cultivate a high number of very diverse components or inclinations in very different ways, combining, feeding into each other also in different ways. A world of very low and very high entropy respectively. These are the kinds of images I hope to evoke, and I shall certainly refer to the first image as that of a highly undeveloped system. Obviously, "development," then, means complexity and balance rather than singlemindedness and growth.

For nature space this is just another way of evoking again the image of conditions for ecological stability. *But nature is a brutal place.* There are certainly exchange cycles, ecological cycles starting with water, carbon dioxide, and solar energy and ending with water and carbon dioxide (solar energy just going on and on, as that bountiful and seemingly endless input). Some of these cycles when translated in a normative manner into rules of behavior in the human, social, and global spaces, would not fare well as models: I am thinking of cycles including the food chain with the "higher" levels consuming the "lower" ones; microorganisms feeding on abiota; plants, also on microorganisms; animals being not only herbivores but also carnivores; human beings feeding on everything but not appreciating the idea that anybody should feed on us, not even ourselves, stamping it out as cannibalism. Obviously, we need another principle here in addition to the idea of symbiosis as generally conceived of:

we need *a principle of respect for the needs of the other.* Exchange cycles, yes, but with some basic form of *tolerance.* In some religious systems this tolerance norm is formulated as *ahimsa,* nonviolence—extended not only to human beings, but also to animals (the case for vegetarianism, in Hinduism and Buddhism), in some cases also to plants and even microorganisms (in principle, the case of Jainism). That was Gandhi's way.

Similarly, at the level of human space in a less biological sense, this means respect and tolerance for other personalities, and at the level of social space, respect, and tolerance for other types of social organization. So there we are, in the midst of philosophical and political wilderness; we are unable to arrive at any formula without some kind of model injunction, some kind of norm. And this is not the norm of social justice, equality, or even equity. As a matter of fact, the norm may even lean toward anti-egalitarianism since equality may have a tendency to lead to uniformity, homogeneity, and here the goal is just the opposite: heterogeneity. Moreover, the concept is not distributive between more or less endowed entities—social justice and equality are such concepts. Equity is a more relational concept, referring to the interaction between entities that it should be "equitable," meaning roughly that all parties should get about equally as much out of it). But here there is not even a demand for equity, except in the very basic sense that relations should get about equally as much out of it. But here there is not even a demand for equity, except in the very basic sense that relations should not lead to the elimination of other types.

But does this not mean that we get into a vicious cycle: on the one hand, we are interested in systems that are developed and peaceful, on the other hand, a condition for a system to be developed is that it is already peaceful, replete with tolerance? Yes, there is an element of circularity in the reasoning but that is not necessarily so problematic. The hypothesis would be that once the system has attained a certain level of diversity, for which I assume some level of tolerance to be a necessary if not a sufficient condition, then diversity will generate more diversity. It will feed on itself, so to speak. The result will be a system increasingly resilient, able to withstand injury from within and without. There is a positive dialectic between peace and development in the sense given here to these complex notions.

So, one arrives at the conclusion that the strong human being is one who permits inside himself and herself several tendencies to emerge, develop, and mature. Take Gandhi as an example: the saint and the politician rolled into one, the two interacting with each other in a highly symbiotic way, with neither the saint driving out the politician nor the politician eliminating the saint. And contrast this with the tendencies in so many societies, perhaps particularly modern occidental civilization, to filter human beings into one particular channel where a limited set of propensities are developed as career—promoting and useful for society, teaching a human being to teach himself to suppress other inclinations. Of course, that person also has what might pass as a way out, segmentation of the inclinations, being one person at work, a totally different person in the family, and still a different person in his or her leisure/happy/peer group life. There is something schizophrenic in this, easily traced back to the formula of missing exchange cycles, of no interaction between the homotopes within that human being. He or she may pay dearly: according to some theories, the price for suppression of important inclinations inside oneself, striving to emerge and develop, may be cancer in somatic terms, schizophrenia or other forms of mental disorders in psychical terms.

From here to *social space* there is but a short step: a

strong society according to this type of thinking would mix
sociotopes and put them creatively together in exchange cycles.
It would not be based on market mechanisms only or planning
only, but on both. It would not be based on centralism only
or decentralization only, but on both. Moreover, it might
be based on all of the above. And the net result, of course,
is a society with a much stronger level of economic/political
activity than found in most "developed" countries today,
combining a capitalist and socialist sector, both at the local
level and the more macro level of social organization. The
green, the blue, and the red together—but only to the extent
that they tolerate each other, in relatively soft forms, in other
words, light green, light blue, and light red! Economic articulation both at the local and the national levels, both as market
and as plan. Political articulation, both as local, direct democracy and national, indirect democracy; both as a mechanism
for selecting leaders or delegates and as a way of having
everybody participate, seeing participation as one possible
input, the output of which is not only social but also human
development.

But what about *world space?* Where do we have a theory
of this type at the global level? Curiously enough, the closest
we come to that is probably the Soviet theory (of the 1930s)
of "active and peaceful coexistence between the two systems."
The idea is that socialism and capitalism can "coexist" at
the global level; in other words, that the world may have
more than one sociotope, and that the coexistence should
be "active," meaning symbiotic; and "peaceful," meaning
tolerant. In other words, the two components from ecological
thinking and the moral injunction, the three principles
together, are all found in the Soviet formula! But having
said that, three critical remarks should immediately be put
forward:

(1) If this is such a good theory for the world, why not also use it *inside* society? Why not have, inside the Soviet Union, some capitalist and some socialist republics—even if this might mean changing the name of the country? (Incidentally, it should be noted that this is what the Chinese now seem to be aiming at with their famous "one country, two systems" formula.)

(2) Why should there be coexistence only between *two* systems? Why not between different systems, not assuming that capitalism/socialism exhausts the range of human imagination? (It does not.) Or, is this fixation on the number two a part of the Manichaean fascination with dichotomies, in Russia particularly well-known as Bogomilism?

(3) Moreover, is this a theory for a goal state of the world or only for a transition to a world with only one sociotope, socialist countries? Is it simply a formula of convenience because capitalism is still too strong and not yet sufficiently in crisis to dig its own grave? Besides, could it be that there is much to learn, e.g., capitalist technologies, which may be useful for socialist countries?

In spite of the validity of these three objections, the formula no doubt points to something very important. And, the formula shows that there may be a basis for convergence of thought not only between the four spaces as here indicated, but also between ideological camps in the world today, combining the avowed tolerance/pluralism of capitalist/liberal societies with some of the thinking of the socialist camp.

REPRODUCTION OF SYSTEMS

Let us then proceed to the sixth column of the table: reproduction, making use of system maturity. In a sense there is nothing new that is being said here. It is only pointed out that if in *nature space* the two conditions are satisfied, then there is a natural renewal capability that is threatened when diversity and/or symbiotic capacity diminish. Similarly, it is pointed out that the same applies in *human space*. It obviously applies to reproduction based on two homotopes, man and woman and their symbiotic interaction, intercourse. Precisely because this is so trivial, it bestows some validity on the scheme. The very condition for the reproduction of human space in a biological sense is already there. The theory touches ground in a very basic sense, so to speak. But this also applies to recovery, from states of ill health. The thesis would simply be that the human being who has grown in diversity, letting the various homotopes in himself/herself play together has a much higher resistance capacity to disease, an immunity system way beyond that which is attributed to the white blood corpuscles. The highly one-sided sportsman dies from overexertion of the heart in middle age; the intellectual who never in any way takes care of his body does the same. Balance is the key to health, but that is but another word for letting more than one human flower grow and interact inside yourself.

When we then move on to *social space,* the logic is the same. A society playing on both market forces and planning forces is stronger provided it has obtained not only a balance in a quantitative sense but also symbiosis in an interactive sense between the two. It is stronger both because of the synergy coming out of that interaction, with planning exercising mild guidance of the market and undoing some of the damages resulting from its social Darwinism, at the same time as the market energizes the planning including the point, sometimes, of giving it something to plan! But there is the second factor: if one of these should fail, for instance because the foreign market collapses or the planning becomes too rigid, there is always the second one. Walking on two legs being better than walking on one; walking on three legs being still far better when one includes the local basis of the economy. And the polity. Actually, this whole approach even yields a theoretical basis for democracy, for what is democracy if not exactly the symbiotic interaction between diverse parties?

It should be noted that both conditions, as well as the moral injunction, are among the pillars on which democracy is based. If there is no diversity, but only uniformity, homogeneity, not only in terms of attitudes/beliefs but also in terms of actions/structures within the confines of a society, then what is the use of interaction? And if there is only pluralism in attitudes and in the sociotopes, (the substructures found inside the social system) but no interaction between them, then one may of course get democracy in the sense of counting prevalences, majorities among the actors, individual and collective. But one does not get the full richness of the system based on give and take, learning and teaching, rubbing attitudes, actions and structures against each other, developing dialectically together, respecting the right of the other attitude and the other actor to exist (but not maintaining them artificially either). In short, not only sexual reproduction and love, but also the whole basis for democratic thinking are already embedded in this simple little approach. Again, that is taken as a confirmation of its validity.

Given these characteristics of a society, reconstruction should in principle come easy. The whole system is vibrant, organic. Hit at some point, there may be injury but there is plenty of material around, even abounding, for reconstruction. And in principle the same applies to the *global space:* the more uniform and devoid of interaction, the more vulnerable; the more diverse and symbiotic, the more capable of reconstructing itself.

RESILIENCE OF SYSTEMS

This is where columns seven and eight enter the picture: the heading they have in common is "Resilience," to direct violence and structural violence respectively, in the columns referred to as "Violence" and "Exploitation." Direct violence is injury to needs, and injury to interests of more complex systems in social and global spaces, meaning their capacity to satisfy the needs of their members. I have defined needs in a very broad sense, including both somatic and nonsomatic needs, and both those that are easily hurt by direct violence and those that are touched by the slow operations, usually unintended, of structures. At the most basic level, this gives us the four major types of injury in the world today: the negation of survival, known as "holocaust"; the negation of well-being, known as "silent holocaust," or structural holocaust as it may also be called—the dying out of people and the cutting off of young human flowers, infants, and small children in the third world; the negation of freedom known as the KZ and the Gulag; and the withering away of feelings of identity to the point where the only focus of identity is one's own ego, one's own needs, not to mention greed—in other words the "spiritual death" of materialist individualism. Systems with high levels of maturity would have the resilience making them capable of resisting such injuries, surviving intact.

Column eight, exploitation, takes up the same theme but in a more basic way. It goes deeper. The injury is no longer only to one particular need (or at the more complex levels, interest) but to the very capacity for reproduction. My definition of "exploitation" is then as follows: any utilization of a resource, in nature, human social or world spaces, to the point where that entity is no longer capable of reproducing itself. In *nature space* it is well known what this means: resources have been made use of beyond their renewal capacity. The result is known as depletion. In *human space* it is also known what this means: a human resource is made use of beyond its production capacity as an individual: it is simply "exhausted." A good night's sleep after sufficient food constitutes some basic conditions for recovery even from serious strain, even from injury. One indicator of what is happening would be to take note of the state of the human body, mind and soul, every morning, over time, until it is quite clear that recovery is no longer taking place. However, the human reproduction capacity from one generation to the next is extremely resilient, so exploitation in human space is ontogenetic rather than phylogenetic, to put it that way. Biogenetic transmission is robust.

A society no longer able to reconstruct itself is a society deprived of its capacity for autonomous reproduction. There is injury to the interests, there is insufficient capacity to undo the injury. In *world space,* this also occurs, civilizations are known to be born, mature, expand and then contract, becoming senile before they eventually die. The metaphor chosen by Naipaul for India, "a wounded civilization" is an apt one. However, it may not apply to India, given the extreme resilience of that particular civilization, and this is evidence by a very simple indicator: its existence on earth for about 3,500 years, which is already more than can be said about most other civilizations.

Injury to reproduction capacity does not necessarily mean death. Reproduction is self-generated, autonomous; but inputs may also come from the outside if the system is not closed. *Nature space* may be artificially kept alive through manure and pesticides; *human space* through biochemical and other types of engineering; *social space* through "development assistance" and "loans"; *regional space* in the same way, as today is being done to the third world. A condition, of course, is that there are other entities in the four spaces capable of extending this assistance. The outcome is probably, in general, that the "woulded system" disappears as an autonomous system and is incorporated into a super system in which the donor is a part, taking on some of the characteristics of the donor. In other words, as an autonomous system it is dead.

MAINTENANCE AS A GOAL OF SYSTEMS

And that brings us to the last column. What is the goal of this entire maintenance exercise? The goal is not system maturity as such, this is rather a condition on which to build. For *nature space* the goal is ecological stability, meaning a system on which human beings can also draw as a resource without hurting its reproduction capacity. Maturity is a condition for this stability. But stability goes beyond, it has to be nurtured and developed further.

In *human space,* one might stipulate a similar goal: health in the broad sense of that word, a sense of somatic, mental, and social well-being as it is quite well expressed by the World Health Organization. Again, system maturity is a condition on which health can be built, somatic health, mental health, spiritual health—the latter usually known as "human development" in a more narrow sense. Or "salvation," in a religious sense.

And the same applies to *social space.* System maturity

only indicates conditions for development to take place. It is like a solid foundation, the rock bottom on which taller structures can be erected. At the same time it gives some ideas about how the construction should take place: in a spirit of pluralism. If there are more ideas around, why not practice several of them, not only one; why not let them interact with each other? The history of civilizations seems to indicate more than clearly that it is the moment, when the rulers think that they have developed *the* only correct idea and put it into practice with a social order with only one sociotope, that the end of that civilization is in sight.

3. SOME CONCLUDING WORDS

This is not the place to develop these themes further, these are only some notes. Let me point out again what many might look at as a weak building block in the construction: "the moral injunction." I see no way of escaping from it, I see no engineering that can guarantee a built-in respect for that which is different. It is something that has to be cultivated, which means that the culture must encourage this type of tolerance as a tenet of belief, one that may survive for a long time. Here, of course, Hinduism and India enter as examples with almost incredible resilience at the level of the social and global spaces. In the other two spaces health and ecological balance are fundamentally not only threatened but eroded—on these spaces tiny, singularistic, and intolerant Norway may be doing better.

In conclusion, let me also point out that the development concept proposed here, *system maturity,* is less growth-oriented and more resilience-oriented. The goal is strength and not at the expense of others, in all four spaces. The approach is holistic. In the growth-oriented approaches, the goal is also strength, but if necessary, at the expense of others, and in a very one-sided way, based on a narrow band of factors only—locating both cause and effect in economic aspects of social space. The result is spectacular until one-sidedness and growth lead to ruptures, decline, and fall.

On the other hand, there is more than enough to do within the present approach—only it is more qualitative and less quantitative. Ecological balance, health, development, and peace—four aspects of development in a broader sense—are not modest goals to be set for oneself, even if there should be some similarity in the underlying logic.

Contributors

SIR HERMAN BONDI is professor of applied mathematics at the University of London, a Laureate of the Academy of Humanism, and a contributor to *Free Inquiry* magazine.

VERN BULLOUGH is dean of natural and social sciences at the State University College of New York at Buffalo, and co-secretary-general of the Academy of Humanism's Secretariat. He is a frequent contributor to *Free Inquiry* magazine.

JOHN GALTUNG is professor of sociology at the University of Oslo, Norway, founder of the International Peace Research Institute of Oslo, and a Laureate of the Academy of Humanism.

PAUL KURTZ is professor of philosophy at the State University of New York at Buffalo, chairman of the Committee for the Scientific Investigation of Claims of the Paranormal (CSICOP), editor of *Free Inquiry* magazine, and founder as well as co-secretary-general of the Academy of Humanism.

GERALD A. LARUE is professor emeritus of archaeology and biblical history at the University of Southern California at Los Angeles. He is chairman of *Free Inquiry* magazine's Committeee for the Scientific Examination of Religion, and a member of the Academy of Humanism's Secretariat. He is a frequent contributor to *Free Inquiry* and has co-edited its annual conference papers.

JEAN-CLAUDE PECKER is professor of astrophysics at the College de France, Academie des Sciences, and a Laureate of the Academy of Humanism.

ALBERTO HIDALGO TUÑON is president of the Asturian Society of Philosophy at Oviedo, Spain, and a Laureate of the Academy of Huanism.

SVETOZAR STOJANOVIĆ is professor of philosophy at the University of Belgrade, Yugoslavia, and a Laureate of the Academy of Humanism. He is a member of the Praxis Group whose members were noted for their defense of democratic freedoms behind the Iron Curtain.

G. A. WELLS is trained in German, philosophy, and natural science. He is professor of German at Birkbeck College, London, a Laureate of the Academy of Humanism, and chairman of the Rationalist Press Association.

www.ingramcontent.com/pod-product-compliance
Lightning Source LLC
Chambersburg PA
CBHW021825090426
42811CB00032B/2028/J